POLLUTION

Jack Gillett with Meg Gillett

Hodder & Stoughton

A MEMBER OF THE HODDER HEADLINE GROUP

Acknowledgements

The authors and the publishers would like to thank the following for permission to reproduce copyright photographs in this book: Life File, Figure 1, Figure 1.3.1, Figure 1.3.2, Figure 2.2.1, Figure 2.2.2, Figure 2.3.3b, Figure 3.5.2, Figure 4.3.4e, Figure 4.3.4f, Figure 5.3.3; Skyscan, Figure 1.3.3, Figure 3.5.1, Figure 3.5.3; PA News, Figure 1.3.4, Figure 3.4.3; Corbis, Figure 1.5.2, Figure 2.3.1, Figure 2.3.5e, Figure 2.4.1, Figure 2.4.4, Figure 2.4.6, Figure 3.3.2, Figure 4.5.4, Figure 5.2.2; J. Allan Cash, Figure 2.3.4b, Figure 2.3.5b, Figure 4.3.4b; mrp photography, Figure 2.3.5c, Figure 2.3.5d; K.K. Kyodo News, Figure 2.4.3; Still Pictures, Figure 4.2.4, Figure 5.3.4; World Health Organisation, Figure 4.2.1; Associated Press, Figure 4.3.4c, Figure 5.2.3, Figure 5.2.5, Figure 5.5.4; Deutsche Luftbild, Figure 4.3.4d; Science Photo Library, Figure 5.3.5; John Noble, Figure 6.1.3; United Waste Services, Figure 6.1.4.

Figure 2.3.6 was provided by Hodder & Stoughton.

The publishers would like to thank The Daily Mail, Manchester Airport and Ordnance Survey (maps reproduced from the Ordnance Survey Landranger mapping with the permission of the Controller of Her Majesty's Stationery Office © Crown copyright; Licence number 399450) for providing copyright materials.

Every effort has been made to contact the holders of copyright material used in this book, but if any have been overlooked the publishers will be pleased to make the necessary alterations at the first opportunity.

Dedication

For Chris, Carol, Helen, Rachel and Jonathan Turner

Orders: please contact Bookpoint Ltd, 39 Milton Park, Abingdon, Oxon OX14 4TD. Telephone: (44) 01235 400414, Fax: (44) 01235 400454. Lines are open from 9.00–6.00, Monday to Saturday, with a 24 hour message answering service. Email address: orders@bookpoint.co.uk

British Library Cataloguing in Publication Data
A catalogue record for this title is available from The British Library

ISBN 0 340 72500 1

First published 1999
Impression number   10 9 8 7 6 5 4 3 2 1
Year   2004 2003 2002 2001 2000 1999

Cover photo supplied by Science Photo Library.
Typeset by Fakenham Photosetting Limited, Fakenham Norfolk NR21 8NL
Printed in China for Hodder & Stoughton Educational, a division of Hodder Headline Plc, 338 Euston Road, London NW1 3BH by Sun Fung Offset Binding Co., Ltd.

Contents

INTRODUCTION

Pollution, like the field of Geography itself, cuts across many related subject boundaries. This book provides a comprehensive introduction to the various causes and environmental implications of pollution; its range of case studies supplies the additional, detailed information required by A and AS level students. The book also provides an insight into many topics of interest to the lay-reader, whose primary aim is to become better-informed about the interaction between human activities and the natural world in which they take place.

Section 1 introduces selected aspects of pollution and should, therefore, be read first! In common with the sections which follow it, Section 1 does not assume any previous relevant knowledge. It may, therefore, be approached in equal confidence by both the lay-reader and the full-time student who may not have opted to study Geography or the three 'separate sciences' to GCSE level.

Sections 2–5 examine four key aspects of pollution within a general spatial progression from the local, through regional and international, to the global scale. Section 2 focuses on the pollution of the lithosphere at a variety of scales, with Unit 2.3 examining some of the issues particularly relevant to resource-based problems. The local issues highlighted by Section 3 mainly concern the lithosphere and the lower layers of the atmosphere. Section 4 acknowledges the fact that water pollution is a matter for concern in a wide range of environments and at a variety of scales. Section 5 examines the primarily global issue of atmospheric pollution.

Section 6 provides an opportunity to consider the likely effects of three potential sources of pollution within a locality in north-west England whilst reinforcing many of the concepts introduced previously by the 'teaching' units of Sections 1–5.

Section 7 provides support material for students whose chief aim is to display mastery of the topics covered within the examination situation. Unit 7.3 may, however, also be relevant to the lay-reader in that it includes a number of questions whose themes extend well beyond the content boundaries of individual units.

The authors hope that readers will make full and regular use of the glossary on page 94. A secure knowledge of the key terms and conceptual themes involved in the study of pollution issues is crucial to genuine understanding and enables the student to respond to examination questions with confidence and from a position of strength.

Readers wishing to extend their knowledge should refer to the recommended book list and selection of Web sites on page 4.

Constructive comments on the format and content of the book are welcomed by the authors; such comments should be directed through the publisher.

Jack and Meg Gillett
Barton, Lancashire

March, 1999

FIGURE 1 The Eiffel Tower, Paris. When this 300 m high iron tower was completed in 1889, it was regarded as a monstrosity by Parisians but is now one of France's most cherished landmarks! Question 2(b) on page 8 invites you to make your own assessment of its 'visual pollution' impact!

Further Reading

An Introduction to Global Environmental Issues
K.T. Pickering & L.A. Owen
Routledge
0-415-14098-6 (hardback)
0-415-14099-4 (paperback)

Environmental Management and Governance
P.J. May, R.J. Burby et al
Routledge
0-415-14446-9

Environmental Science
K. Byrne
Nelson
0-17-448243-4

Environmental Science for Environmental Management
T. O'Riordan (Ed)
Longman
0-582-21889-6

Environmental Science: Earth as a Living Planet
D.B. Botkin & E.A. Keller
John Wiley & Son
0-471-15782-1

Europe's Environment: The Dobris Assessment
D. Stanners & P. Bourdeau (Ed)
European Environment Agency
92-826-5409-5

Global Environment: Water, Air and Geochemical Cycles
E.K. Berner & R.A. Berner
Prentice Hall
0-13-301169-0

Human Systems and the Environment
R. Prosser
Nelson
0-17-444070-7

Living in the Environment
G.T. Miller Jnr.
Wadsworth Publishing Company
0-534-51912-1

Managing Environmental Systems
R. Prosser
Nelson
0-17-448223-X

Natural Systems and Human Responses
R. Prosser
Nelson
0-17-444069-3

The Complete A-Z Geography Handbook
M. Skinner, D. Redfern & G. Farmer
Hodder & Stoughton
0-340-654899

The North Sea
M. MacGarvin
Collins & Brown
1-85585-005-2

Understanding Our Environment: An Introduction to Environmental Chemistry and Pollution
R.M. Harrison (Ed)
Royal Society of Chemistry
0-85186-233-0

Who's Who in the Environment: England
S. Cowell (Ed)
The Environment Council
0-903158-35-3

Acid Rain Information Centre	http://www.doc.mmu.ac.uk/
BBC News	http://news.bbc.co.uk/
British Nuclear Fuels	http://www.bnfl.co.uk/
Commission for New Towns	http://www.cnt.org.uk/
Countryside Commission	http://countryside.gov.uk/
English Nature	http://www.english-nature.org.uk/
Environment Agency of England and Wales	http://www.environment-agency.gov.uk/
Financial Times	http://www.ft.com/
Forestry Commission	http://www.forestry.gov.uk/
Friends of the Earth	http://www.foe.co.uk/
Greenpeace	http://www.greenpeace.org.uk/
The Guardian	http://www.guardian.co.uk/
International Monetary Fund	http://www.imf.org/
Powergen	http://www.pgen.com/
The Times	http://www.the-times.co.uk/
UK Atomic Energy Authority	http://www.ukaea.org.uk/
UK Department of the Environment, Transport and the Regions	http://www.detr.gov.uk/
UK Department of Trade and Industry	http://www.dti.gov.uk/
United Nations Development Programme	http://www.undp.org/
World Bank	http://www.worldbank.org/
World Conservation Monitoring Centre	http://www.wcmc.org.uk:80/forest/data/
World Health Organisation	http://www.who.ch/

1
PERSPECTIVES ON POLLUTION

1.1 Towards a definition of 'pollution'

Pollution is one of the increasingly dominant themes of modern times; most people are now not only generally aware of what is meant by 'pollution', but are also able to quote a range of examples of its impact on the life of this planet. The dedicated student of pollution-related matters does, however, need to be very clear about what is understood by the term, as well as precisely what is involved in the pollution process.

In the 1980s, pre-graduate students were often given some credit simply for quoting the term *pollution* in examination answers – because doing this could be viewed as introducing a separate, 'mark-worthy' theme. In the early 1990s, examiners began to regard the use of the word alone as being far too vague to justify credit. In effect, the term *pollution* had become just as commonplace and imprecise as *good* and *ideal* – OK to use, but of real value only if supplemented with detailed information! The requirement for increasingly precise term usage continues and current examiners of post-GCSE students now regard even longer terms such as *air pollution* and *noise pollution* as purely introductory. This book therefore emphasises the importance of accurate term usage just as much as the need for detailed information about pollution processes and the case-study situations which result from them.

The following selections of definitions for 'contamination' and 'pollution' illustrate the degree of flexibility with which people often use these two key terms.

Definitions of 'contamination':

■ The presence of an undesirable material which makes something unfit for use;
■ A process by which something becomes impure, defiled, dirty or otherwise unclean;

■ The presence of increasing concentrations of substances in water, sediments or organisms.

Definitions of 'pollution':

■ The occurrence of an unwanted change in the environment caused by the introduction of harmful materials or production of harmful conditions (e.g. significantly higher levels of heat and sound);
■ An event which adversely affects the health of organisms or their environment;
■ An interference which disturbs environmental processes;
■ A harmful effect on the environment caused by human activity and involving noise, dirt and poisonous substances;
■ An undesirable change in the physical, chemical or biological characteristics of air, water, soil or food which can adversely affect the health, survival or activities of humans or other living organisms.

STUDENT ACTIVITY 1.1

1 (a) Discuss, within small groups, the individual merits of each of the above definitions for *contamination* and *pollution*, then agree what you consider to be the most appropriate 'general' definition of each term. You may opt to retain or amend existing definitions, but it is probably more likely that you will to wish to draft original alternatives! (b) Write down your 'perfected' definitions of both terms.
2 Also as a result of group discussion, argue the merits of the statement: 'Contamination and pollution are *not* the same; contamination is, however, a necessary first stage in the more general process known as pollution'. Summarise the chief points raised by your discussion.

1.2 Basic principles

All group-activities tend to create new terms which, initially, are quite specific to those activities. In due course, regular usage of the more widely-applicable of these terms allows them to become integrated into the basic vocabulary of the more general community. This unit defines some of the more important environmental terms which have now passed into common usage. An awareness of these 'standard terms' is most important, for the reasons listed below:

■ because they have generally-agreed yet precise meanings, they aid effective communication and minimise the risk of confusion between groups of people engaged in similar activities;
■ they avoid the need for repetitive, lengthy and often imprecise descriptions of core concepts;
■ they can aid policy implementation, because their meanings are accessible to policy-implementers as well as policy-initiators;
■ they enable us to structure current knowledge in a logical and coherent way;
■ they also aid the development of new philosophies upon which future developments may be based.

The following standard terms define concepts which have dominated environmental debate in recent decades. Familiarity with these terms is therefore crucial to a genuine understanding of the topics discussed in this book.

Built-in obsolescence A manufacturing strategy which *ensures* that products have a relatively short life-span. This involves the use of materials of limited quality and quantity, thus increasing the volume of production and, ultimately, company profitability. This strategy is, however, extremely wasteful of the world's finite reserves of industrial raw materials. A classic example of built-in obsolescence was car production in the 1960s, few examples of which now remain because of rapid body-rusting and early component-exhaustion. In complete contrast, total rejection of the built-in obsolescence principle by Rolls-Royce has allowed 60 per cent of all cars produced by that company since its formation in 1904 to remain in existence *and still be in a road-worthy condition!*

Cost-benefit analysis is a means of forecasting the social and economic costs of a new development. It involves an assessment of likely environmental damage as well as any predictable economic benefits. The former is *much* more difficult to achieve with any degree of accuracy, but the necessary assessment techniques are being constantly refined and are usually based on the monitored consequences of past developments.

Development Any initiative intended to achieve cultural, economic or social 'improvement'. An earlier concept of development focused on purely economic matters, such as changing rates of industrial and agricultural production, and was often used to assess the relative wealth of individual countries. The current concept is more broadly-based, so as to include other major aspects of human endeavour.

Ecosystem A term first used in 1935, as an abbreviated form of 'ecological system'. An ecosystem is a community of plant and animal life within the context of its physical environment. An example is given in Figure 1.2.1. Ecosystems may incorporate one or more of the following earth components:

■ **biosphere** (or **ecosphere**) – that component in which living organisms exist and interact both with one another and their abiotic (non-living) environment. It includes most of the hydrosphere, parts of the lower atmosphere and sections of the upper lithosphere;
■ **hydrosphere** – that component which includes water, in all its liquid, solid or vaporous forms;
■ **lithosphere** – the earth's crust and upper mantle (Figure 1.2.2). The crust contains minerals, non-renewable fossil fuels and the nutrients essential to plant and animal life.

LEDC Economically less developed country, i.e. one whose economic growth has not been as rapid as that of the long-industrialised countries. LEDCs often used to be referred to collectively as '**The Third World**'.

MEDC Economically more developed country.

Recycling is the re-use of materials which would otherwise be discarded and so no longer be available as a human resource. Glass, paper and iron/steel are relatively easy to recycle. Non-ferrous metals such as aluminium, copper and lead are especially valued re-cycling commodities due to their scarcity. Recycling makes environmental sense because:

FIGURE 1.2.1 Ecosystem components

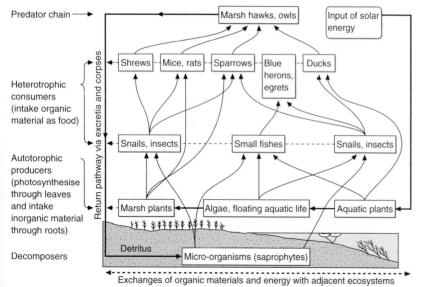

- it conserves **finite resources** (i.e. those whose *accessible* reserves are strictly limited);
- the process of mineral extraction often involves widespread visual and noise pollution, as well as the **degradation** (significant reduction in quality) of the earth's natural components;
- recycling existing materials is usually a much less energy-intensive process than the initial extraction of minerals from their ores;
- less land has to set aside for the disposal of discarded materials.

Self-sufficiency describes a community's ability to provide all that is needed for its long-term survival. Examples of true self-sufficiency are now very rare, as hitherto fully self-sufficient communities such as the Amazonian tribes, the Bushmen of the Kalahari Desert in southern Africa and Australian Aborigines have become increasingly dependent on goods and services obtainable only through closer contact with their more developed neighbours. Whilst most self-sufficient communities are **land-intensive** (i.e. require comparatively large amounts of land), their traditional respect for the limitations of local environments ensures that these do not become degraded by total reliance upon them. 'Modern' societies, on the other hand, have become completely dependent on technologies which demand constant injections of additional natural resources – hence the increasing popularity of sustainable development policies.

Sustainable development is a concept very closely allied to that of self-sufficiency. Its fundamental requirement is that any new development should meet the needs of the present whilst not compromising the ability of future generations to meet their own needs. It does *not* imply that human activity should become 'fossilised' in the present – just that its demands on limited global resources should be modest and have a long-term perspective. A prime example of sustainable development would be re-afforestation programmes on a scale which is comparable to that of the current demand for new timber products. The principle of sustainable development may be applied to all aspects of human activity, in both rural and urban contexts, and at scales ranging from major international developments to the most modest of local initiatives. The concept of sustainable development was first proposed by Harlem Brundtland, a past Prime Minister of Norway, in *Our Common Future* published in 1987 by the World Commission on Environment and Development (WCED). It was subsequently adopted as a key theme of the 1992 Rio de Janeiro Earth Summit discussed in Unit 5.4.

The precautionary principle, as its name suggests, advocates great caution when interpreting scientific information about the state of the environment. In essence, it requires that any development which involves a significant risk of environmental damage should, ideally, not be allowed to proceed. Where such developments are regarded as 'essential', they should be undertaken on as reduced a scale as possible *and* incorporate the maximum possible safeguards. The precautionary principle was first advocated in *The World Environment*, published by the United Nations Environment Programme (UNEP) in 1992. It has since become a key aspect of the European Union's overall environmental strategy and is a guiding principle behind maritime restoration programmes for the North Sea region.

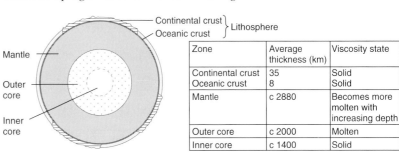

Zone	Average thickness (km)	Viscosity state
Continental crust	35	Solid
Oceanic crust	8	Solid
Mantle	c 2880	Becomes more molten with increasing depth
Outer core	c 2000	Molten
Inner core	c 1400	Solid

FIGURE 1.2.2 Internal structure of the earth

STUDENT ACTIVITY 1.2

Produce your own Glossary of the terms highlighted by bold type in this unit; your definitions for these terms can be quite brief!

1.3 *Visual pollution*

The growth of scientific knowledge allows us to identify and then quantify, with increasing accuracy, most forms of pollution and their impact on the earth's natural environments and ecosystems. The events listed in Question 1 represent only a tiny fraction of the number of such impacts, but they do give some indication of both their great diversity and the global nature of pollution.

The notable exception to the increasing application of scientific knowledge is 'visual' pollution – chiefly because its assessment is a highly *subjective* process, based on an individual's own perception and judgement of what is acceptable.

While such arbitrary decisions are often made very quickly (e.g. when viewing an exceptionally ugly factory pouring smoke into the atmosphere!), they are frequently much more subtly-based – using criteria determined solely by a person's own cultural and experiential background.

Question 2 below invites you to refine a given set of criteria for assessing visual pollution. You should, however, only attempt this exercise after reading the following observations. Imagine the following components: a steam-powered train travelling through a wooded piece of countryside. An environmentalist's response might involve the following questions:

■ does the train track blend in or conflict with its natural surroundings?

■ is the train itself a visually attractive feature?

■ do the smoke and steam produced by the railway engine add to or detract from the visual quality of the scene?

■ do these emissions into the atmosphere trigger off concerns about their likely impact on the environment?

These five questions do, of course, represent only one set of **criteria** by which the existence of visual pollution within the chosen scene may be judged; you may feel that this set can be refined or extended in some way, to make the assessment process much more rigorous. The chief purpose of the last question is to challenge the observer to consider any non-visual factors which might influence the overall assessment; as environmentalists often instinctively respond to non-visual factors when making such judgements, it would seem appropriate to include at least one criterion designed to incorporate the non-visual. Another refinement – allowing some quantifiable follow-up work to be undertaken – would be to allocate a range of score responses within a carefully-graded scale (e.g. of 1–5), so that the answers to all the criteria-based questions could be assessed on an equal basis. The same technique could be applied to a range of scenes and so make quantified comparisons of the varying degrees of visual pollution within it.

FIGURE 1.3.1 Visual pollution near Williton in Somerset

STUDENT ACTIVITY 1.3

1 (a) Add the following brief summaries of pollution-related incidents to their correct locations on an outline map of the world:

■ *In East Anglia (England)*, 'Insurance premiums are forecast to rise sharply due to the increased risk of houses flooding as a result of global warming';

■ *In Erfjord (on the Norwegian coast)*, 'Brent Spar, a disued 14 500 tonne North Sea oil platform, was cut into six sections to become ferry quaysides – to avoid it being sunk in the Atlantic where it could have caused serious water pollution';

■ *In Antartica*, 'The ship *KRISTA DAM* collected thousands of tonnes of oil drums and other waste material left by past Antarctic expeditions';

■ *Close to Jamaica*, 'Large sections of coral reef destroyed by offshore pollution in the Caribbean Sea';

■ *In Western Australia*, 'Open-cast mining of iron ore causes widespread visual, noise and air pollution in the Hammersley Range';

■ *Indonesia*, 'Large tracts of tropical rain forest destroyed by fires caused by land clearance';

■ *Along the River Danube*, 'Nitrates and phosphates from farms in Austria and Germany caused algae blooms to form, killing off millions of fish and rendering extinct up to 40 entire species of fish';

■ *In California*, 'In January, 1997 floodwaters released some of the 7600 tonnes of mercury used during the 1849 Gold Rush to dissolve the gold flakes from their parent rock. Mercury levels 160 times the seasonal average recorded immediately after the flood';

■ *At the entrance to Tokyo Bay, (Japan)*, 'In July, 1997 the supertanker *DIAMOND GRACE* ran aground on a shallow reef and broke into two sections. Over 13 000 tonnes of her cargo of 257 000 tonnes of crude oil escaped into Tokyo Bay'.

(b) Now add at least a further three *more recent* examples of pollution to your world map. This could be done at a later stage, as suitable opportunities arise.

2 (a) Discuss whether, and how, the five assessment criteria listed on this page could be improved so as to make the assessment of visual pollution more effective.

(b) Use your list of 'improved' criteria to assess the degree of visual pollution in each of the scenes in Figures 1.3.2–5 and the view of the Eiffel Tower shown on page 3.

FIGURE 1.3.2 Wheal Coates tin mine ruins, Cornwall

FIGURE 1.3.3 Sydney
Opera House, Australia

FIGURE 1.3.4 'Angel of
the North' (52m), erected
in 1998 next to the A1 (T)
south of Gateshead, Tyne
and Wear

FIGURE 1.3.5 An example of British motorway 'architecture' near Birmingham

1.4 Contrasting city environments

Every country experiences pollution problems of some kind or another. The nature and severity of an individual country's problems are the direct result of a wide range of factors; historical legacies, industrial practices, the nature of transportation networks and the general level of wealth as indicated by **Gross Domestic Product** (GDP) are just four of the most important of these factors. Unfortunately – and perhaps surprisingly, as well – there is little firm evidence to suggest that increasing wealth *always* results in reduced pollution. In fact, some of the poorest agricultural countries (especially those in sub-Saharan West Africa) have quite low levels of pollution, while the industrially and scientifically highly successful USA is currently one of the world's most serious air polluters! In other words, money and knowledge alone are not the most vital **prime movers** in pollution reduction. It is the timely combination of adequate knowledge, technology, and finance plus the determination to achieve reductions which is crucial. All too often the determination factor is lacking, simply because short-time priorities such as a healthy profit on a company's annual balance sheet or a local authority's eagerness to keep next year's rates as low as possible are perceived to outweigh much longer-term environmental benefits. This book examines a number of such failures, as well as some very encouraging examples of attitudes which have been changed by the sustained efforts of **non-governmental organisations** (NGOs) such as Greenpeace.

Question 1, below, invites you to describe (but not explain!) the contrasting pollution patterns in two cities which have very different climatic conditions and cultural backgrounds. Later activities in this unit focus on some of the reasons for the widely differing pollution levels which occur throughout the world, particularly the on-going burden of **national debt** (often referred to on the Internet as **foreign** or **external debt**).

FIGURE 1.4.1

	Bangladesh	Malawi	Mozambique	Nicaragua	Tanzania
GDP per capita ($)	219	133	93	409	115
National debt ($ million)	16 083	2312	5842	5929	7412
Population (millions)	120	10	16	4	30
National debt per capita ($)	134	231	365	102	247

STUDENT ACTIVITY 1.4

1 Study the information in figure 1.4.1 very carefully, but do *not* attempt to plot it using graphical means!

(a) What major patterns within the tabled information are you able to detect *purely by eye*?

(b) Assess the likely implications of the patterns which you have just identified for these countries' ability to finance significant reductions in pollution.

FIGURE 1.4.2 Pollution problems in Karachi, Pakistan

Karachi's environmental problems

The number of eagles circling just above the ground give an impression of thriving wildlife, but this is Karachi, Pakistan's largest and **primate city**, where these flesh-eating birds thrive by feeding off corpses deliberately left out on hillsides called 'Towers of Silence', set aside for that very purpose. When the eagles' work is done, the bare bones are buried elsewhere with traditional respect for the dead. The eagle (and rat) populations also act as the city's dustmen – by removing waste food from domestic refuse.

In the early morning, the sun does not seem to shine until it is well above the horizon – even though the sky is usually cloudless. In fact, the sun *never* attains its full strength in this city of 10 million people, because of chronic atmospheric pollution; local concentrations of sulphur dioxide alone are three times higher than the World Health Organisation's estimates of what is considered safe. The city's human population is growing at a rate of 750 000 per year, in spite of the lack of adequate water supply and sewage disposal systems. Due to the total absence of controls on vehicle exhaust emissions, central Karachi appears to be permanently foggy, and the **life expectancy** of its street traders is consequently very short.

The haze is partly caused by the city's thermal power stations, which burn 'furnace oil' imported from the Persian Gulf. This is regarded as the world's dirtiest fuel and its use without the most stringent emission controls is banned in all Western European countries. Karachi's existing power stations emit highly poisonous fumes and the environmental **degradation** caused by them is estimated to cost Pakistan at least £1 billion every year. Yet there are plans to build another five similar stations, to provide the Karachi area with 24-hour access to electricity; these plans do not incorporate any form of pollution abatement equipment – even though they too are to burn the cheap furnace oil.

Large numbers of Karachi's workers die prematurely every year because of inhaling emitted particles which build-up in their lungs. In addition, as much as 25 per cent of the total industrial workforce are already totally or partially deaf due to exposure to excessively noisy machinery. A recent Environmental Protection Act makes industrial pollution of any kind an offence which can attract fines of up to £100 000, but corruption is endemic throughout Pakistan; this makes it very easy for influential employers to avoid prosecution and punishment – even in the most serious cases.

The city's swamps are green with algae, and water pollution has reduced the number of species of mangrove within them from eight to only one in the last 30 years. The shrimp industry, which uses the swamps as a nursery, and the local fishing industry are both threatened with extinction by the release of 2500 tonnes of raw sewage into the river Lyari each day.

The lives of many thousands of people are believed to be especially at risk from pollution in the densely-populated Karachi district of Malir – as a result of fumes and leakages from a government dump for pesticides which have been discarded because they are out-of-date. These are stored in containers which are becoming so weathered that they seem highly likely to leak in the near future. Local officials are particularly concerned for the safety of children at two schools in the area; they believe that increased temperatures and humidity (both regular features of the summer months) will make these pesticides so unstable that they will produce toxic fumes capable of killing the children. The Malir dump is just one of many similar dumping sites across Pakistan and it is estimated that over 5000 tonnes of condemned pesticide currently await final disposal.

FIGURE 1.4.3 Pollution problems in Krakow, Poland

Krakow's environmental problems

Satellite photographs of Eastern Europe show the world's largest airborne tumour – a dense patch of industrial gas and dust which completely blots out the easterly Renaissance city of Krakow, in Poland. Its situation in the valley of the River Wista means that locally-generated air pollution accumulates and becomes highly concentrated. Within the lifetime of just one generation, polluted air has eaten into the faces of its many sandstone statues.

From Poland's Karkonosze Mountains, it is possible to smell the usually tarry but occasionally sulphurous air. The snow in southern Poland is so acidic that it has killed most of the trout in local streams and entire tracts of once-glorious pine forest are now reduced to a landscape of ugly stumps. According to the Polish Academy of Sciences, only 17 per cent of the country's vast woodlands have escaped serious ecological damage.

Immensely rich in lignite (often called 'brown' coal), Poland has suffered environmentally as a direct result of the Soviet obsession with industrial growth in the 1960s. Modern demands were placed on what was largely pre-war – and even nineteenth century – technology. Because of this, Polish factories still consume up to three times as much energy as those in Western Europe; they also emit between 10 and 20 times as much pollution. For at least the last three decades, the 'acceptable level' of pollution created by a steel plant or copper mill was regarded as that created by meeting ever-increasing production quotas! Iron foundries, steel mills, chemical plants, coal mines, coke works and towering waste heaps are often sited close to workers' houses and the air is so filthy that people have acquired the habit of drying their laundry in attics. Gardens and allotments are regularly dusted with fresh layers of soot and it is unwise to walk under trees because their leaves are often similarly coated. Special warning maps alert gardeners and farmers to the most heavily polluted areas, where concentrations of lead within the soil may be as high as *900 times* the accepted safety level. Lead fumes from crudely-refined petrol inhaled by local children have produced three times the incidences of hyperactivity, memory loss and mental re-

tardation which are common in the surrounding rural areas.

The most common local air pollutant is sulphur dioxide – the chief ingredient of **acid rain**. Poland 'imports' much of its sulphur dioxide from nearby Germany and the Czech Republic, but in a typical year the country exports far more than it receives! Much of the 4.3 million tonnes which Poland produces every year circulates within the country's boundaries. The principal source of sulphur dioxide pollution is Polish coal, as it is used very widely by industry, the major power stations, municipal central heating systems and individual homes. It also yields benzo-alpha-pyrene (BAP), one of the deadliest of all **carcinogens**. Poles are acutely aware of the health hazards created by benzo-alpha-pyrene, as it is one of the major factors in the doubling of childhood leukaemia within a period of only 13 years. The air is so laden with BAP that it is constantly tainted with the acrid smell usually associated with chemistry laboratories!

Since 1970, overall life expectancy in Poland has *fallen* – down to its 1950 level. Polish children are now far less healthy than their parents and grandparents; more children are being born with physical and mental handicaps, and their subsequent state of health appears to deteriorate very rapidly. In Katowice, 70 km west north west of Krakow, 50 per cent of all four year olds experience chronic illnesses; by the age of 10, 75 per cent of them are so unwell that they require regular medical treatment.

Many of Poland's rivers are now biologically 'comatose'. The Vistula, Poland's main waterway, is so chemically active for 80 per cent of its length that it is unfit even for industrial use as it is quite capable of corroding the machinery. Some 10 000 factories sluice their unfiltered effluent into it and half of the 800 or so communities along its banks do not possess sewage treatment plants. The Vistula conveys 90 000 tonnes of nitrogen, 5000 tonnes of phosphorous, 80 tonnes of mercury and further quantities of cadmium, zinc, lead and copper into the Baltic Sea – where fish are so scarce that the Polish fleet can catch only 20 per cent of its allotted quota.

STUDENT ACTIVITY 1.5

1 (a) Use the information about pollution in Karachi and Krackow given in Figures 1.4.2–3 to complete an enlarged version of the table below. For each of the five listed categories, you will need to outline the nature of its chief pollution problems and summarise their effects on the local human, flora and fauna populations.

(b) According to your completed table, what appear to be the chief similarities and differences between the pollution characteristics of these two cities?

1.5 *Natural pollutants*

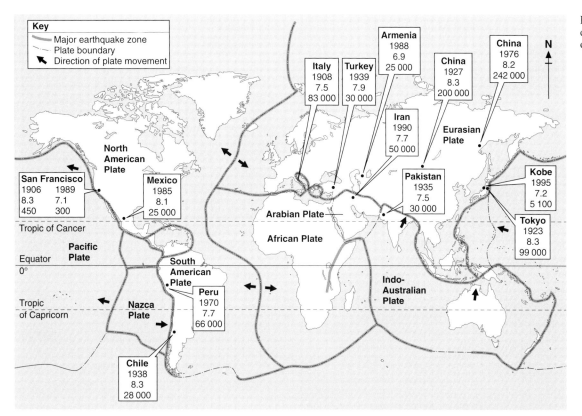

FIGURE 1.5.1 Distribution of the world's chief areas of volcanic activity

Many of the processes and all of the case studies referred to elsewhere in this book are the direct result of human activity. This unit examines two types of occurrence which result from the earth's own natural cycles.

Volcanic activity

Volcanic activity on the earth's surface is triggered by weaknesses within the uppermost layer (the crust); these points or lines of weakness allow pressurised **magma** from the mantle beneath to escape (after which it is termed **lava**!). Relatively fluid forms of lava are able to flow some distance before they cool sufficiently to form layers of solid rock. More viscous lavas solidify much closer to their point of emergence; they 'pile-up', to form mountains having the familiar cone-shape of a volcano. The emerging lava may be accompanied by emissions of steam, sulphur-laden gases and fine ash – creating a period of brief but intense air pollution. These acrid gases are capable of

FIGURE 1.5.2 The 1883 Krakatoa volcanic eruption, Indonesia

STUDENT ACTIVITY 1.6

1 Describe and explain the distribution of those regions which are most susceptible to volcanic activity.
2 Summarise the *pollutant* effects of volcanic activity.

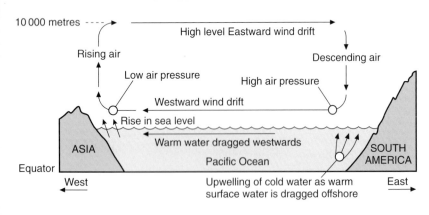

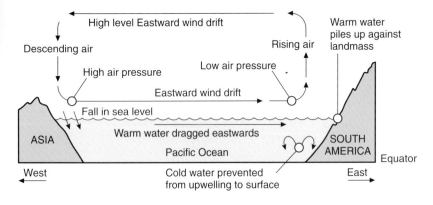

FIGURE 1.5.3 'Normal' atmospheric and maritime conditions in the Pacific Ocean region

---

STUDENT ACTIVITY 1.7

1 Use Figures 1.5.3 and 4 to describe those abnormalities which initiate the El Niño phenomenon.
2 Outline separately the purely environmental and non-environmental effects of El Niño.

FIGURE 1.5.4 'Abnormal' atmospheric and maritime conditions in the Pacific Ocean region giving rise to El Niño formation

devastating whole farming areas by 'burning-off' their crops and pasture.

A volcano becomes dormant when any magma remaining within the escape pipe solidifies and prevents further upward flow. This may cause the trapped magma to become so pressurised that it blows off the entire volcanic peak, shattering it and ejecting the entire mass of fragments into the atmosphere to leave behind a hollow remnant called a caldera. In the most extreme cases, this airborne debris may be carried thousands of kilometres by global wind 'belts'. Such cataclysmic eruptions may produce spectacular sunsets over great distances for a number of years; they can also create fogs so dense as to make life unbearable in down-wind settlements and prevent sunlight reaching productive arable farming areas. Figure 1.5.1 highlights the regions most at risk from volcanic activity and includes summaries of some of the most dramatic volcanic explosions of the past.

'El Niño'

'El Niño' (a Spanish name meaning 'the Christ child') is another entirely natural phenomenon. Its origins are in the Pacific Ocean, yet its devastating effects are felt well beyond the Pacific coastline. It does not, however, follow a regular, annual pattern, but tends to occur at intervals of between two and seven years. The most recent occurrences were in 1982–3, 1991–2 and 1997–8. El Niño – which produces abnormally warm Pacific currents – is sometimes followed by a potentially equally destructive counter-phenomenon called El Niña. The latter is triggered by *sub*-normal surface temperatures in the same region and is linked to instability in the permanent mass of cold water above the ocean floor.

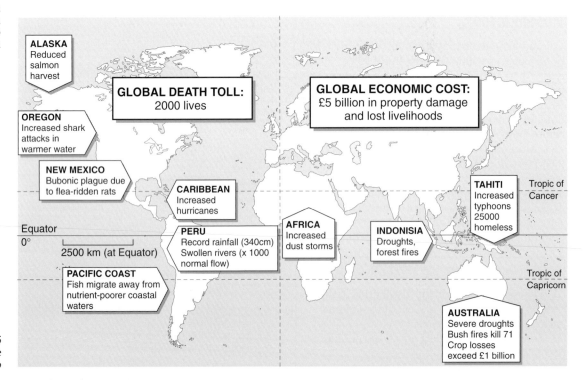

FIGURE 1.5.5 Consequences of the 1997–8 El Niño

2

LAND POLLUTION — *THE ECONOMIC DIMENSION*

2.1 Land-use factors

In 1798, an English economist, the Reverend Thomas Malthus, published '*An Essay on the Principle of Population as it affects the Future Improvement of Society*'. Its purpose was to investigate possible links between changing population and the availability of resources needed to support such changes. He concluded that unchecked population growth is most likely to accelerate at an **exponential (geometric) rate**, whilst any increase in the production of food could, at best, be expected to take place at a much more consistent, **arithmetic rate**. He was later proved to be somewhat over-pessimistic with regard to food production. He did not foresee the impact of the agricultural revolution which transformed European food production during the nineteenth century; neither could he have predicted the successful development of new colonial farmlands – particularly in North America and Australasia – which induced large-scale migration from the already over-populated regions of Western Europe.

Although focusing on the matter of food production, Malthus' essay did alert its readers to the more general challenge of meeting *all* the requirements of a growing and increasingly demanding population. The most basic human needs also include water, clothing, shelter, energy for heating and cooking and (increasingly) transportation – all of which place escalating and often conflicting demands on available resources.

The global population 'explosion' of the mid/late twentieth century has placed many regions well beyond the population *optimum* (in that they can no longer provide adequately for all their people); it has also led to a depletion of many key resources and the widespread degradation of natural environments.

To many, it remains both inconceivable and inexcusable that it should be possible to 'plunder' vital natural resources in the pursuit of short-term and often localised goals. It is also difficult to accept that planning controls designed to restrict the speculative and often haphazard use of land are a quite recent innovation in most countries. The following units examine three contrasting types of land-use development; they also illustrate the escalating pressures placed upon available land by the need to meet the demands of expanding populations and advancing technologies.

STUDENT ACTIVITY 2.1

1 (a) Describe the changing pace of global population growth illustrated in Figure 2.1.1.

  (b) Utilise your answer to (a) above to assess the accuracy of Malthus' prediction of population growth.

2 Suggest the most likely benefits of strict planning controls in areas of increasing population and resource pressures.

Year	Global population – in millions	Year	Global population – in millions
1750	771	1950	2525
1800	954	1975	4066
1850	1241	2000	6100 (estimated)
1900	1634		

FIGURE 2.1.1 Global population change 1750–2000

2.2 The Agricultural Revolution

The second half of the twentieth century witnessed a comprehensive revolution in agriculture – a revolution which transformed farming activities throughout the world. The list below is not exhaustive, but does include some of the most fundamental and widespread changes which took place during that 50-year period.

■ increased mechanisation, which enabled farming to be less labour-intensive whilst becoming much more productive;

■ the amalgamation of farms; also the consolidation of small, dispersed parcels of land which had become fragmented (widely separated) over time into much larger and therefore potentially more viable and efficient agricultural units;

■ the increasing influence of wholesalers and retailers in dictating quality standards and the supply of food products in most demand;

■ the adoption of '**agribusiness**' techniques, which have put farming in MEDCs on a much more systematic and profitable basis;

■ the widespread use of 'intensive' farming methods, such as broiler houses for increasing poultry and egg production;

■ increased governmental and international intervention – a notable example being the European Union's 'Common Agricultural Policy', which established subsidies to encourage and reward increased productivity – leading, inevitably, to overproduction of cereal crops and milk;

■ the '**green revolution**', which transformed agriculture in many LEDCs by providing extra irrigation facilities and developing higher-yielding crop strains;

■ the development and increased use of synthetic applications such as fertilisers to increase crop yields and reduce wastage caused by disease and natural preditors.

This 'harvest hymn' by the English poet John Betjeman (1906–84), which is a *parody* of *All Things Bright and Beautiful*, provides a rather sardonic view of the modern farmer's approach to his work – but there is more than a grain of truth in what it has to say!

> *We spray the fields and scatter*
> *The poison on the ground*
> *So that no wicked wild flowers*
> *Upon our farm be found.*
> *We like whatever helps us*
> *To line our purse with pence;*
> *The twenty-four hour broiler house*
> *And neat electric fence.*

Chorus: All concrete sheds around us
> *And Jaguars in the yard,*
> *The telly lounge and deep freezer*
> *Are ours from working hard.*

> *We fire the fields for harvest,*
> *The hedges swell the flame,*
> *The oak tree and the cottages*
> *From which our fathers came.*
> *We give no compensation*
> *The earth is ours today*
> *And if we lose on arable,*
> *Then bungalows will pay.*

Chorus: All concrete sheds . . .

FIGURE 2.2.1 'Traditional' British farming landscape

FIGURE 2.2.2 'Modern' British arable farming landscape

STUDENT ACTIVITY 2.2

1 Use the list of trends given on this page, Benjamin's poem and Figures 2.2.1 and 2.2.2 to outline the major changes which have taken place in farming practices in recent years.

The chief groups of farmland applications are:
- **fertilisers** such as nitrogen, phosphorus, potassium and calcium, all of which are essential to plant growth;
- **fungicides** such as dithiocarbamates and diazines;
- **herbicides** such as substituted ureas and triazines;
- **pesticides** (especially **insecticides**) such as organophosphates and chlorinates hydrocarbons.

The rest of this unit examines the impact of two of the most important types of farmland applications, which have collectively posed the greatest pollutant threat to rural environments.

Focus on fertilisers

Farmland may be fertilised in a number of ways. **Organic** fertilisers occur naturally, by the decay of plant remains and animal urine and faeces. The fertilising of fields by this natural process can be accelerated by adding slurry from animals kept indoors; also by using crop rotation systems which allow nitrate-hungry crops such as wheat to be seasonally alternated with certain other crops (e.g. sugar beet and oil seed rape) which restore nitrogen levels within the soil. Increasingly, **manufactured** fertilisers are being used to boost natural nitrogen inputs (Figure 2.2.3).

Any excess quantities of nitrogen within the soil are leached by rainfall into adjacent drainage systems. Nitrogen, in the form of nitrates, is highly soluble. Because of this, nitrate concentrations in streams and reservoirs closely follow any changes to the quantities applied to nearby farmland – especially in highly porous, sandy soil areas from which groundwater can drain very quickly. The close link between quantity of fertiliser applied and nitrate-concentration within field boundary ditches was demonstrated very clearly immediately after the British drought of 1976. Widespread crop failures following an exceptionally dry Spring and Summer had allowed the concentrations of unused nitrates to build-up in the soil – until flushed out by the heavy rainfall in the September and October of that year which ended the drought.

A similar situation occurred after the exceptionally hot summer of 1989, when increased quantities of phosphorus entered many of the reservoirs in East Anglia and prompted such rapid growth of algae (microscopic plants) that their recreational use had to be suspended until more normal concentrations were achieved.

The Food and Environmental Protection Act of 1985 made it compulsory to report the use of artificial applications such as fertilisers; regular reporting and careful monitoring have increased our understanding of the environmental consequences of their use. However, nitrate concentrations well above the EU limit of 50 milligrams/cubic litre are still commonplace within the more vulnerable British regions (Figure 2.2.4).

High levels of nitrate in water pose a serious threat to both humans and marine life-forms. Young children are at particular risk – from a condition known as methaemoglobinaemia, which reduces the capacity of the blood to carry oxygen around the body and in extreme cases may prove fatal. Concentrations of more than twice the EU permitted level could induce **carcinogens** in the stomach.

On entering streams or lakes, high-nitrate water concentrations disturb the existing delicate ecological balance – initially due to the increased activity of bacteria and fungi, whose primary function is to break down waste materials, consuming more dissolved oxygen and raising ammonia levels within the water as they do so.

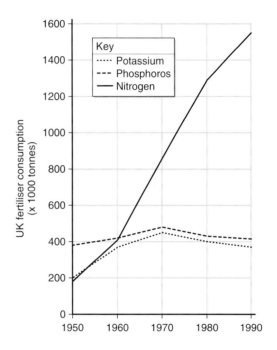

FIGURE 2.2.3 Selected British fertiliser usage trends: 1950–90

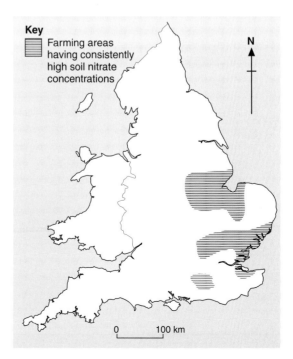

FIGURE 2.2.4 Variations in nitrate concentrations within British soil

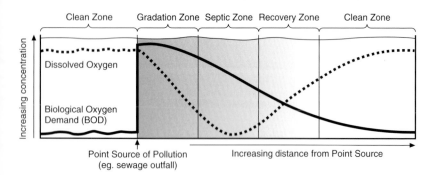

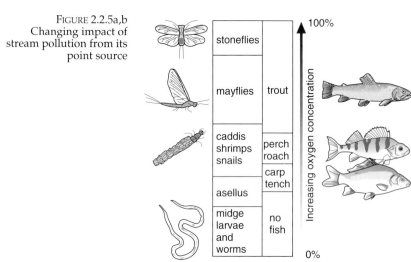

FIGURE 2.2.5a,b
Changing impact of
stream pollution from its
point source

FIGURE 2.2.6 BOD
investigation technique
for use with Question 8

Continued de-oxygenation kills off the fauna (fish population) and increases the cloudiness of the water, thus preventing light from filtering down to submerged flora. The subsequent death and decay of this plant life releases hydrogen sulphide – a pungent gas which is a sure indicator of water which has already been heavily polluted through this process of **eutrophication**.

Figure 2.2.5 traces the effects on the flora and fauna of a typical stream from the **point source** of pollution. One of the diagrams in Figure 2.2.5 shows how the vital oxygen content within the water changes with increasing distance from the point source. It similarly tracks changes in the **biochemical oxygen demand** (BOD) – another important statistic which is a measure of the ability of organic effluent to de-oxygenate water at a particular location within the stream. BOD is quite easy to calculate, using the technique illustrated in Figure 2.2.6.

BOD tests may be undertaken using oxygen-measuring probes or one of the dissolved-oxygen test kits available from scientific equipment wholesalers. The following sample collection and storage guidelines should be followed carefully:

■ Local environmental conditions have a considerable influence on dissolved oxygen content, which tends to increase with lower water temperatures and (at sub-surface levels) with higher wind speeds;

■ As photosynthesis takes place continuously during daylight, comparative readings at intervals along a stream should be taken simultaneously;

■ Take at least 10 samples from each distance interval from the point source of pollution.

■ Take samples at a range of depths well below the surface and above the stream bottom;

■ Allow some overflow from sample bottles and fill to the rim prior to sealing so as to minimise the risk of trapping bubbles;

■ 'Fix' samples in bottles immediately after collection;

■ Store samples well away from bright light, by using dark glass containers or wrapping clear containers with masking tape – this prevents photosynthesis replenishing the oxygen content during storage;

■ Keep bottled samples in a constant, room temperature (20°C is best).

Each sample must be tested for dissolved oxygen content twice: first as soon as possible after collection and again after five days. Both readings are taken in 'milligrams per litres'. The final stage is to subtract the second mean reading from the first and interpret each difference as follows:

1–2 mg/l: ('very good')

3–5 mg/l: ('moderately clean')

6–9 mg/l: ('moderately polluted')

10 mg/l and above: ('very polluted')

STUDENT ACTIVITY 2.3

1 Write down the correct terms for the five types of artificial farm applications in common use, adding its definition (from the Glossary on page 94) and at least one example of each type.

2 Summarise the environmental effects of the two climatic events mentioned in the text. What actions might have been taken to reduce these effects.

3 Using information from Figure 2.2.3, construct a table which has these four column headings:

Fertiliser	Quantity used in 1970	Quantity used in 1995	Percentage increase in use between 1970 and 1995*

*Use this formula to obtain the data needed for the last column:

$$\% = \left(\frac{1995 \text{ quantity} - 1970 \text{ quantity}}{1970 \text{ quantity}} \right) \times 100$$

4 (a) Describe the distribution pattern of high nitrate concentrations shown by Figure 2.2.4, naming the chief areas involved as far as possible. (b) With the help of atlas maps, suggest reasons which help to explain the distribution pattern you have just described.

5 Summarise the potential effects on the human body of high nitrate concentrations in drinking water.

6 Describe the process of eutrophication within a stream subjected to inputs of nitrate-enriched water. Refer to Figure 2.2.5 as well as the text.

7 Carry out a series of experiments, using Figure 2.2.6 as your guide, to investigate changing BOD levels along part of a water course in your local area. Show your findings in an appropriate graphical form, then draw conclusions from the data which you have illustrated in this way.

Focus on pesticides

'Pests' are members of any species which competes with humans for food; rodents such as rats and mice and insects (e.g. locusts) form major pest categories. At least 50 per cent of all pests are kept in check by their natural preditors within ecosystems, but the losses caused by these preditors are so great that artificial means have been sought to reduce them. Chemical pesticides are by no means a recent innovation; sulphur was used as early as 500 BC and the widespread application of arsenic, lead and mercury since the thirteenth century was abandoned only as recently as the 1920s – when it became clear that they were also hazardous to humans! In 1939, an entomologist called Paul Mueller discovered DDT's potential as an effective pesticide and its use was swiftly adopted by most major countries.

About 25 000 different manufactured pesticides are now available to farmers, the great majority of them being relatively safe to humans as they are derived from chemicals which are produced naturally by plants. Many of these pesticides have low persistence within ecosystems, although DDT is one of a small range which can remain active within natural ecosystems for up to 15 years. The application of pesticides is justified on the grounds that they prevent the loss of some 55 per cent of world food production, either before harvesting or during later transportation and storage. They act speedily and are considered to be a sound investment because they may save up to four times their cost in lost production, particularly when the 'broad-spectrum' varieties (which can target a much greater range of pests than the more selective agents) are used in a single application.

The use of pesticides is not without risk; organophosphates are especially toxic to humans and most reported poisonings have been traced to their mis-use. The newspaper article in Figure 2.2.7 highlights one common activity which has been a source of concern to sheep farmers for many years – the practice of dipping animals in chemical solutions to protect their flocks against pests which cause intense discomfort and often prove fatal. The new dip solution has been developed to replace many older forms which are now proved to attack the human nervous system – with some very distressing results to long-term users. It is certainly more user-friendly but is now shown to have a devastating effect on the local environment if not disposed of correctly. The development of increasingly potent applications is, however, constantly required as their pest targets are usually able to build up increased tolerance.

Many individuals, notably the Prince of Wales, have advocated **organic farming** as the most effective way of maintaining the natural balance in agriculture areas. Major food retailers have responded to the increased public demand for organic produce.

STUDENT ACTIVITY 2.4

1 (a) Quote figures from the text which appear to justify the large-scale use of manufactured pesticides.
(b) Outline some of the major difficulties associated with the use of such pesticides.
2 Undertake your own investigation into the methods used in organic farming and the ways in which supermarket chains have promoted food produced by this means.

FIGURE 2.2.7 Source: THE INDEPENDENT, 22 November, 1997

Sheep-dip pollution prompts crackdown

Upland farmers carelessly disposing of a new kind of sheep dip are wiping out life in mile after mile of rivers and steams. *Nicholas Schoon*, Environment Correspondent, says that the Government's Environment Agency has plans to crack down on the polluters.

Both coarse and game fishermen are calling for the SP dips to be withdrawn. They can also cause problems when the wool from dipped sheep passes through processing and cleaning plants – their effluent can harm rivers. The Environment Agency is talking to the textile industry about tackling that.

Grampian Pharmaceuticals, which sells most of the SP dip in Britain, said that provided the instructions accompanying the product were followed there should be no damage. It had sent details of the code of practice to all 8000 of its customers.

In Cumbria alone, about 145 km of river have been damaged by the new synthetic pyrethroid (SP) sheep dips leaking into the water.

The chemical wipes out most of the tiny aquatic insects, crustacea and other invertebrates near the base of the food webs. This starves the fish and that, in turn, deprives otters and river birds of their fish food. Streams have also been harmed in upland areas of the West Country and Wales.

SP dips have been marketed as a safer alternative for ridding sheep of parasites than the organophosphate dips which have caused severe, chronic illness in many farmers. Sales have soared over the past five years. But according to the Environment Agency, they are up to one hundred times more lethal to river life, and a teaspoonful entering a stream can wipe out invertebrates for hundreds of metres downstream.

Farmers are currently asked to follow a code of good practice when they dispose of surplus dip. This allows them to pour it onto flat grassland, provided it is at least 10 metres from any river and 50 metres from any well or borehole.

The European Commission believes that this is inadequate, and is prosecuting Britain for failing to comply with EU water pollution laws. The Government has responded by promising new regulations to come into force next year.

Source: *Independent* 22 November 1997

2.3 Rock and Mineral Extraction

FIGURE 2.3.1 China clay workings near St Austell, Cornwall

petroleum and natural gas fields. Whilst different in many respects, all three activities do share the same unfortunate tendency to disfigure the landscape. Some generate large quantities of 'waste', whose disposal is a major contributor to visual pollution. It is, for example, quite usual for waste rock to form at least one-third of all material brought to the surface from shaft (underground) coal mines. A more extreme case is the china-clay workings of south Cornwall, from which the ratio of waste to clay is 9:1 (Figure 2.3.1). Even petroleum extraction is environmentally hazardous, as the initial drilling processes involves the removal of rock, soil and drilling muds; leakages of these muds and the oil itself can seriously contaminate the immediate area around the boreholes.

Visual pollution is increased by the dereliction of abandoned buildings and the deterioration of discarded machinery. Weathering over many years has mellowed some relics of the extractive industries to the extent that they now form tourist attractions and have even been accorded protective 'listed building' status (see Figure 1.3.1). These are rare exceptions, however, and the great majority of Britain's derelict quarrying and mining sites represent both major environmental failures in the past and restorative challenges for the future.

Extractive primary industries have always had a serious impact on the natural environment. They frequently result in considerable short-term disturbance, followed by permanent disfiguration of the landscape. The adverse effects of mineral extraction are particularly striking because of the scale of the workings involved, their ability to transform the visual appearance of localities and the tendency for extraction companies to quit worked-out sites as quickly and as cheaply as possible. The increasing effectiveness of planning regulations and sustained action by environmental lobbies have done much to accelerate site restoration in recent years. However, the scarring legacies of the industrial past are often very difficult to erase.

The sections in this unit are devoted to three key aspects of extractive primary industry: stone quarrying, coal mining and the exploitation of

Quarrying

The construction industry cannot function without constant supplies of newly-excavated materials; recycling (e.g. of builders' rubble from demolition work) does provide some useful hardcore, but the quantities involved are quite small in comparison with total annual requirements (Figure 2.3.2). Most of Britain's 1200 quarries operate to meet local or regional needs – due to the high cost of transporting such bulky, heavy and relatively cheap materials by road or, more cost-effectively, by rail and water. Certain materials (e.g. potash from the coastal area around Whitby in North Yorkshire) are of national significance and their scarcity often proves to be a crucial factor in the granting of planning permission. Material-intensive developments such as the construction of motorways and airports may also sway planning authority decisions in favour of granting approval; on average, some 100 000 tonnes of sand, gravel and chippings are required for every kilometre of new motorway and cost considerations often dictate that these materials be obtained within a very modest transportation radius.

Rock quarrying is especially disruptive of the local environment. Whilst some jobs are created by the quarrying industry in rural areas having few alternative employment opportunities, there is usually a heavy price to be paid in terms of congestion on local roads and pollution by the noise and dust created by blasting and crushing

FIGURE 2.3.2 British unemployment and rock-output trends: 1980–96

Year	UK annual extraction of building materials (millions of tonnes)	UK unemployment (% of total workforce)
1980	233.4	4.75
1981	210.8	8.16
1982	225.2	9.47
1983	245.5	10.93
1984	239.2	10.62
1985	243.1	10.89
1986	250.5	11.19
1987	277.5	10.14
1988	311.8	8.11
1989	319.1	6.29
1990	296.3	5.64
1991	218.0	8.08
1992	200.4	9.59
1993	204.8	10.33
1994	229.1	9.38
1995	212.2	8.22
1996	191.2	7.63

operations. Some of the most heated planning debates surrounding quarry mineral exploitation have taken place in areas of great scenic value. Such conflict resulted in the original boundary lines of two British National Parks being re-routed to exclude localities where environmental disfiguration was already considered to be unacceptably severe (Figures 2.3.3 and 4).

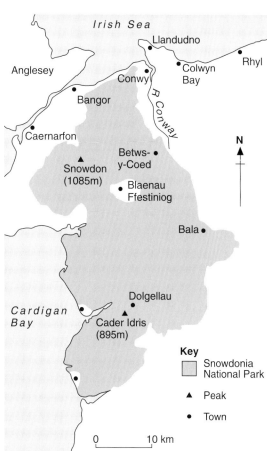

FIGURE 2.3.3a Snowdonia National Park
FIGURE 2.3.3b Abandoned slate quarry at Blaenau Ffestiniog, North Wales

FIGURE 2.3.4a Peak District National Park
FIGURE 2.3.4b Limestone quarry near Buxton, Derbyshire

STUDENT ACTIVITY 2.5

1 Debate, then justify or refute, the statement 'Quarrying should be regarded as one of the most environmentally-damaging primary industries of modern times'.

2 To what extent is it likely that serious environmental hazards *always* accompany major quarrying activities? If possible, you should support your views by referring to quarry sites with which you are familiar.

3 (a) Summarise then comment on the patterns of construction materials extraction illustrated in Figure 2.3.2.

(b) Describe and then suggest reasons for the apparent relationship between the construction material extraction and unemployment trends shown by Figure 2.3.2. Plotting a 'double-line' graph may help you to do this.

4 With the help of Figures 2.3.3 and 4, describe briefly where and how environmental considerations have influenced the routing of British National Park boundaries.

Coal mining

Coal seams may be exploited either on the surface (by open-cast mining) or by deep shaft-mining techniques. Underground mining pollutes the working environment and silicosis continues to be a major health risk – in spite of modern spraying techniques which trap much of the dust generated by mining machinery. Surface mining involves ripping up the **overburden**, but permanent physical damage to the environment can then be alleviated to some extent by sensitive landscaping. The tall winding gear associated with shaft mining is often visible from considerable distances and inevitably disfigures what might otherwise remain highly attractive rural landscapes.

Recent British coal mining developments have incorporated a range of measures designed to minimise landscape disfigurement. Such measures have become a crucial part of company development plans and are the product of statutory consultation with local communities and environmental protection groups during the planning enquiry process. The Selby Coalfield development first produced coal in 1983 – *16 years* after its discovery – following an intense period of heated debate. Provided local scenery and historic buildings were safeguarded the scheme was permitted to proceed. Figure 2.3.5 highlights the chief protective measures taken to safeguard the rural environment in this locality south of York.

STUDENT ACTIVITY 2.6

1 Use the information in Figure 2.3.5 to outline some of the environmental protection measures adopted in the Selby Coalfield development.

FIGURE 2.3.5a Selby Coalfield, North Yorkshire

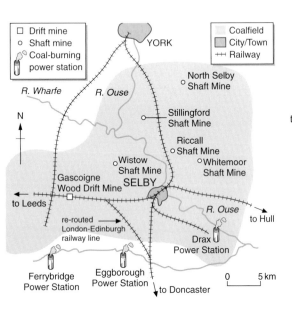

FIGURE 2.3.5d Shaft Mine. Any waste material brought to the surface at the five shaft mines and the one drift mine is tipped around the mine site, landscaped and planted with trees

FIGURE 2.3.5b Selby Abbey, under which a broad pillar of coal was left unworked to protect its delicate eleventh century foundations

FIGURE 2.3.5c Gasgoine Wood Drift Mine – the only point in the entire coalfield area at which coal is brought to the surface; less countryside is disfigured by siting railway sidings and coal stockyards in just one locality. The drift mine method of extracting coal avoids the use of tall winding gear which would spoil distant views across the surrounding countryside

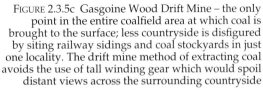

FIGURE 2.3.5e River Ouse, whose banks were raised by the (then) National Coal Board to reduce the risk of adjacent farmland being flooded

Oil exploitation

Because of its fluidity, highly volatile nature and importance in international trade, crude oil (petroleum) has come to be regarded as the most environmentally-threatening of all the fossil fuels. This is partly due to major pollution incidents such as the accidental running aground of the *SEA EMPRESS* (Unit 4.4), which have traumatised local wildlife habitats and attracted media attention for lengthy periods of time. Less dramatic but continuous 'operational discharges' occur in the normal course of exploration, extraction, transportation, processing and final disposal of crude oil and its many by-products. Figure 2.3.6 shows the relative importance of the different categories of oil spillage in recent years.

Oil is a highly complex mineral – a combination of thousands of different organic molecules, many of which are extremely toxic. It is chiefly composed of hydrocarbons, with smaller quantities of sulphur, oxygen and nitrogen impurities. Aromatic oils tend to disperse more rapidly than the heavier oils – mainly by evaporation, bacteria-aided breakdown and dissolution within the water. These processes occur more rapidly in warmer environments; stormy conditions are also helpful in aiding dispersal and degradation, as was proved by the *BRAER* incident, when exceptionally violent local weather conditions greatly reduced the environmental impact of her 87 000 tonne discharge.

Oil residues which remain after natural degradation of the lighter components has taken place often coagulate into less toxic but very unsightly 'tar balls'. These may float on the surface for anything up to a year before being washed ashore or totally degraded out at sea. Oil slicks – continuous deposits which blanket the water surface – will coat any form of wildlife unable to escape their movement over the surface. Offshore bird communities and wildlife restricted to the inter-tidal coastal region are at greatest risk. Sand and gravel shores are also highly vulnerable, due to oil's ability to seep quickly and deeply through these types of beach material.

The risk of environmental pollution from oil spillages increases dramatically in times of armed conflict; static installations such as pipelines and land-based extraction rigs are especially vulnerable to enemy action or attack by local groups of 'guerilla' fighters. During the Second World War, it was standard practise to target major oil facilities – action which inevitably had serious adverse effects on marine and atmospheric environments. During the 1990–1 Gulf War, Iraq deliberately set alight hundreds of wells to deny oil to Desert Storm forces, creating fires and smoke palls which took many years to overcome (Figure 2.3.7).

At sea, oil tankers have always been highly-prized targets of submarine captains and large numbers of both British and Japanese tankers were sunk during 1939–45, their damaged hulls spilling entire cargoes onto the surface. Fortunately, many such sinkings took place well out to sea, where wave and wind forces could disperse their spillages relatively quickly. Other maritime targets added very considerably to the pollution effects of the war at sea; the ruptured fuel tanks of British submarine casualties alone (only a tiny fraction of the total warship losses) accounted for spillages far greater than those from the *BRAER* and *SEA EMPRESS* incidents added together.

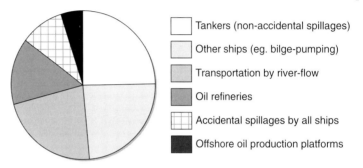

FIGURE 2.3.6 Sources of maritime oil pollution

- Tankers (non-accidental spillages)
- Other ships (eg. bilge-pumping)
- Transportation by river-flow
- Oil refineries
- Accidental spillages by all ships
- Offshore oil production platforms

STUDENT ACTIVITY 2.7

1 Outline the major environmental hazards associated with the exploitation of oil resources, referring to specific named examples as appropriate.

FIGURE 2.3.7 Kuwaiti oil wells set on fire by Iraqi forces during the Gulf War of 1990–1

2.4 Industrial Waste

FIGURE 2.4.1 Steelworks

Industrial pollution may be caused inadvertently (by accidents which occur despite precautionary measures taken to prevent them), or by ongoing waste-disposal procedures adopted by companies. A number of case studies exemplifying the former cause are discussed fully in other units; the purpose of this unit is to examine two outstanding examples of the latter.

Industrial waste may enter the environment in a variety of ways. Solid wastes are frequently disposed of on nearby land surfaces, where they may either accumulate to levels which make them either visually unsightly or capable of posing an indirect threat to both human and wildlife populations. The dumping of waste into hydrospheric flows and sinks is so common as to also justify inclusion in this unit. Flowing water conveniently transports pollutants away from their source points into seas and oceans, whose natural forces have traditionally been regarded as capable of diluting, degrading and dispersing them quite adequately. Atmospheric pollution is similarly very important and is most commonly caused by gases and **particulate solids** emitted from chimneys. The second case study in this unit deals with one example of air pollution caused in this way.

CASE STUDY

Hydrospheric pollution caused by waste disposal: Minamata, Japan

One of the most-publicised examples of offshore dumping occurred during the post-war period in the industrialised fishing community of Minamata, a town of 35 000 people on the southernmost Japanese island of Kyushu (Figure 2.4.2). The town's name has now become enshrined in environmental history – due to the so-called Minamata Disease which increasingly ravaged its population's health until reaching a peak in the early 1970s. It was caused by the discharge of mercury waste into local fishing grounds within a sheltered bay to the west of the town.

The dangers of inhaling mercury vapour have been known for many centuries. There are well-documented cases of madness amongst nineteenth century hat makers, who constantly used mercury compounds in the treatment of their fabrics – hence the Mad Hatter's odd behaviour in *Alice in Wonderland*! The case in Minamata was somewhat different, as it involved inorganic mercury compounds which, being readily converted biologically into soluble forms, can enter food chains then affect cell membranes within the host's body.

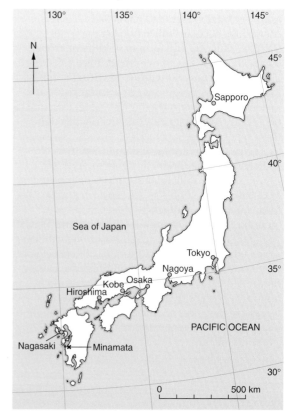

FIGURE 2.4.2 Location of Minamata City, Japan

The existence of major poisoning in Minamata became clear in the years 1953–60, when 111 persons who had recently eaten local fish and shellfish began to suffer numbness of the fingers and toes, deafness, blurring of vision, loss of bodily control and, in the most severe cases, emotional instability. The cause was thought to be a localised but highly infectious disease and it was not until the end of the 1950s that discharges of metallic mercury and dimethyl mercury were proved to be the real cause. It was only in 1968 – *15 years* after the first reported case of poisoning – that the factory involved officially accepted that its own discharges were to blame.

Ever since the conclusion of the Second World War, industrial growth has been vigorously encouraged by successive Japanese governments – to the extent that its national industrial output increased during the 1960s at an annual rate of 15 per cent and its overall GDP by 11 per cent – both exceptionally high figures by global standards. The Japanese workforce was highly supportive of its corporate leadership and, particularly in the earlier decades of this expansion phase, was willing to accept long working hours and some degree of environmental discomfort as necessary to increasing Japan's share of international trade.

A succession of highly disturbing environmental incidents has since forced the Japanese to revise their traditional *laissez-faire* approach to environmental issues, especially in the highly industrialised, densely inhabited districts (DIDs) on the coast. The outbreak of Minamata Disease was one of the most influential of these incidents, which traumatised the Japanese so much that they coined a new word *kogai* as a general term for any form of environmental hazard. Minamata Disease alone resulted in over 2250 fatalities and seriously-ill casualties – 6 per cent of the town's entire population.

Traditionally a fishing village, Minamata was chosen as the site for a factory (Figure 2.4.3) to be built by the Japan Carbide Company in 1908. It was later bought by its successor, the Chisso Corporation, which operates in the petro-chemical industry. In the 1930s, the factory began to produce acetaldehyde – a substance involved in the manufacture of a wide range of products including medicines and perfumes. The waste from their new process was dumped in Minamata Bay, in the form of mercury sludge. As the factory expanded over time, so did the volume of its effluent. After some 20 years of continuous dumping, the inhabitants of Minamata began to witness some very unusual and disturbing sights.

Large numbers of commercially-important fish appeared to be in great distress; entire flocks of sea birds became so weak that even attempting to fly exhausted them; domestic cats began to dance frantically on the streets and by the late 1950s, very few cats remained in and around Minamata City. The local people were certainly curious at what they saw, but not unduly distressed at that early stage.

Their detached and unemotional approach only began to change when some of the human population began to show major symptoms of illness. Medical examinations highlighted paralysis and mental illness as the chief symptoms. Shortly afterwards, mercury waste was proved beyond doubt to be their primary cause (Figure 2.4.4). In some cases, pregnant mothers did not seem to be affected, but later gave birth to children with congenital mercury poisoning.

Minamata proved to be very typical of towns dominated by a single company. Loyalty towards the major source of employment was very strong – even for Japan, where employer-employee ties are traditionally close and become increasingly so over the years. Chisso currently provides 10 per cent of all full-time jobs and about one-third of all engineering jobs in the town. When the real cause of the disease was identified, many citizens were so fearful of factory closure that they tried to have 'Minamata' removed from the name of the sickness! The community was deeply divided over the issues involved and those maimed by the poison were actively discriminated against. For many years, the disease was taboo – far too sensitive a topic and much too embarrassing to discuss openly.

FIGURE 2.4.3 Chisso Petro-chemical Plant, Minamata City

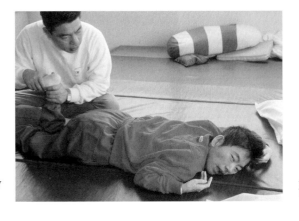
FIGURE 2.4.4 Victim of 'Minamata Disease'

Since 1978, the company's earnings have been insufficient to meet victims' compensation claims and it has only been possible for Chisso to continue in business with the support of bonds issued by Kumamoto Prefecture. Chisso has had to borrow 150 billion yen to compensate medically-certified patients and meet the costs of filling-in the most heavily polluted section of Minamata Bay. It seems doubtful whether Chisso will ever earn enough to refund all its borrowings as well as pay the interest charges on existing loans. In spite of this, the national government has given a firm undertaking that everything possible will be done to safeguard Chisso's survival.

Minamata is now beginning to face the future with much greater confidence. A new environmental centre has been erected on the north side of the reclaimed area and provides information on a wide range of environmental protection strategies. The town is now more honest about its environmental past and actively encourages tourists and industrial representatives to visit it as an example of a 'model environmental town where you can learn about these problems first-hand'.

Minamata's increased openness about its local environmental issues reflects similar changes on a national scale. Japan has consistently allocated more than 2 per cent of its national GDP to internal environmental protection measures and is one of the world's major contributors to international environmental schemes. In 1967, the Diet (the Japanese parliament) passed its first relevant act, 'The Basic Law for Environmental Pollution Control'; and in 1974, 'The Pollution Compensation Law' achieved its primary aim of forcing industrial leaders to accept that it is *their* responsibility to compensate workers whose health is jeopardised by environmentally-hazardous procedures.

More recent legislation has progressively strengthened environmental controls in Japan. However, the financial crisis which first undermined the economies of many south east Asian LEDC countries in 1997 has also had serious effects within Japan. It is highly likely to put Japanese exporters under intense pressure to reduce their production costs and make their goods even more competitive in a reducing world market – an ominous sign for the environmental protection of the Japanese workforce.

CASE STUDY

Atmospheric pollution caused by waste disposal: Sudbury, Canada

FIGURE 2.4.5 Location of Sudbury, Canada

A particularly notorious example of localised air pollution occurred around the nickel-smelting town of Sudbury in the Canadian state of Ontario (Figure 2.4.5). Nickel is a key component in the chemical and electronic industries; it is also used in the manufacture of the especially hard steels fitted to cutting instruments and for protective armour plating; cupro-nickel alloys are highly suitable for 'silver' coinage; because they are so durable.

The Sudbury Basin area is particularly rich in nickel-ore deposits. These lay undiscovered until 1883, when builders of the Canadian Pacific Railway stumbled across surface deposits to the west of the site where the town now lies. Copper was the initial target, as this was found to be the dominant metal in the local ore. In 1891, however, a means of separating the two metals from the same ore was discovered and, during the 1960s, Sudbury rapidly became one of the world's most important sources of nickel; it also became Canada's chief single source of sulphur dioxide pollution! The heating process used to refine nickel also released the core's high sulphur content, producing dense emissions of sulphur dioxide gas. These had such a devastating effect on the surrounding area that it was chosen as a training ground for astronauts preparing for the first lunar landings! (Figure 2.4.6).

STUDENT ACTIVITY 2.8

1   Design a flow-diagram which links the events described in the account of Minamata Disease and its consequences.
2   Outline and add reasons for the changing attitudes of Minamata residents to environmental pollution matters.
3   Summarise and comment on the changing Japanese attitude to environmental matters.

FIGURE 2.4.6 'Lunar' landscape near Sudbury

STUDENT ACTIVITY 2.9

1 Outline the reasons for and nature of the environmental damage caused to the Sudbury area by nickel smelting.
2 Debate the assertion: 'aesthetic rather than environmental considerations were the higher priority in Sudbury's restoration initiatives'.

As a result of decades of SO_2 emission, the forests which clothed the area nearest to Sudbury were utterly destroyed by the resultant acid rain deposits; a 250 square kilometre area was laid completely barren by the atmospheric 'burning' of tree foliage. Somewhat less severe damage took place within a further 3500 square kilometre zone. Increased soil erosion and damage to soil structure were caused by the influx of heavy metal deposits. Copper and nickel concentrations in the soil as high as ten times above the norm have been recorded; soil acidity levels there have ranged from pH 2.0 to 4.5. Vegetation damage was very comprehensive within the most highly polluted areas, as only certain crustose lichens were able to survive within them. Research has established a very close correlation between distance from smelter and the level of environmental damage occurring in a particular location.

Tall smelter stacks were constructed in the late 1960s to accelerate the dispersal of the SO_2 emissions. These did reduce local concentrations by more than 50 per cent, but immediately increased rates of deposition in the more distant, down-wind localities! The Ontario state government laid down standards aimed to reduce annual emissions by 1994 to below 365 000 tonnes – a reduction of 85 per cent on the previous peak figure. This was achieved by reducing smelter production whilst increasing the filtering of stack emissions.

Large-scale tree plantings have since done much to 'green' the devastated landscape and in doing so produce a more natural and aesthetically pleasant environment for the local population. Nutrient and organic matter additions have helped to restore the balance in soil composition. Much of the restoration work was co-ordinated by the Sudbury Environmental Enhancement Programme (SEEP), formed in 1969 as a joint venture between the Ontario Department of Lands and Forests and the Laurentian University Biology Department.

Initial restoration programmes focused on research, the removal of thousands of unsightly tree stumps and re-afforestation programmes in the worst affected areas. As most of the newly planted saplings seemed to die off quite quickly, later programmes concentrated on soil restoration instead. Imported soil was laid over selected areas prior to further planting, but this strategy proved too costly to be adopted on a large scale. A less cost-intensive but more effective approach was to plant only in small pockets of up-graded soil. Lime was however applied very widely, at a rate of about 2 tonnes per hectare – the rockier areas having to be treated by hand. Hardy native conifers were planted extensively, but in 'higher visibility' areas near to the town and its access roads, more colourful species such as sugar maple and red oak were introduced instead. Large areas were grassed over and later used for recreational use.

Student labour was utilised under the auspices of the Young Canada Works Programme and funded by both local and regional governments; YCWP sponsorship alone helped to reclaim 1450 ha of barren land and plant 230 000 trees. Additionally, over 1700 short-term jobs were created – thus weakening a trend towards welfare-dependency caused by the mining redundancies. The total area covered by reclamation initiatives exceeded 60 square kilometres and focused on high-profile areas, transport corridors and residential neighbourhoods. Sudbury's new green image has attracted much investment to the area and so reduced its domination by the mineral extraction and processing companies. Large stretches of countryside remain disfigured and heavily contaminated and it is estimated that, so far, only about 30 per cent of the total seriously-affected area has been adequately restored.

3

URBAN POLLUTION – *LOCAL ISSUES*

3.1 *The migration factor*

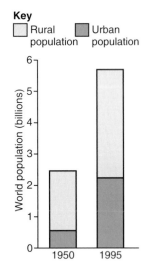

Key
Rural population (light)
Urban population (dark)

World population (billions)

1950   1995

Unit 1.1 introduced the fact that the world's population continues to rise, with the twentieth century witnessing the highest rates of increase within recorded history; it also referred briefly to certain patterns of international migration which took place during the previous century.

The units in Section 3 focus on the environmental impact of **urbanisation** – a phenomenon which continues to dominate settlement patterns throughout the world. In most developing countries, rapid urbanisation has been the product of internal, rural-urban migration, as well as high rates of 'natural population increase', which are the

result of a marked imbalance between the birth and death rates and were a major factor in the population 'explosion' of the mid/late twentieth century. Similar patterns of internal migration continue to occur within MEDCs, but at a much reduced rate. Both categories of country, however, share the same tendency for primate cities to develop at the expense of 'less-attractive', and therefore smaller, settlements. The size factor is highly significant in environmental terms, as larger settlements tend to create more pollution than the mere size of their populations might suggest.

3.2 *Urban 'heat islands'*

FIGURE 3.1.1 Evidence of global urbanisation: 1950–90

The curiously named 'heat island effect' is a localised phenomenon, caused by the additional heat generated by urban areas. It occurs worldwide, though most strikingly in MEDC cities because they are more highly energy-intensive. The phenomenon modifies a range of environmental patterns, the most important being humidity, wind speed, cloud cover, precipitation and air temperature.

STUDENT ACTIVITY 3.1

1 Comment on the information displayed in Figure 3.1.1.
2 What kinds of 'factors' might help to explain the emergence and subsequent long-term dominance of primate cities?
3 *You should not refer to the later units of the book before attempting this question!* Make a list of the likely impacts of urbanisation on both local and regional environments; when doing this, you may find it helpful to make comparisons of different-sized settlements with which you are familiar.

Its choice of name is quite appropriate, because isotherm patterns such as that shown in Figure 3.2.1 for Greater London are similar to the relief contour patterns of maritime islands. The choice of climatic circumstances chosen for London's pattern – an anticyclone on a typical summer evening – is also significant. This is because high air pressure systems bring calmer and more stable atmospheric conditions; strong winds, on the other hand, tend to disperse the modest heat generated by local buildings, factories and transport networks. They also reduce any air movement generated locally by heat and air pressure differentials (Figure 3.2.2). Apart from increased temperature, the Greater London area often experiences wind speed reductions (−6%) and humidity reduction (−5%), whilst increased total annual precipitation (+30%) is caused by more frequent thunderstorms.

Figure 3.2.3 highlights the ways in which the characteristics of a typical British urban area might influence these processes. The nature of the heat island effect in other countries reflects local lifestyles and the choice of construction materials. Central Business Districts (CBDs) in most of the world's primate cities are now very similar – due to the widespread use of high-rise commercial and residential blocks – but many of the older residential zones still use more traditional construction materials such as stone and adobe; these have larger *specific heat* capacities and so retain more of the warmth which they have absorbed during the day. Tropical and sub-tropical zones increase the need for air-conditioning within buildings, but the continuous use of such equipment generates additional external heat – thus adding to the local heat island effect!

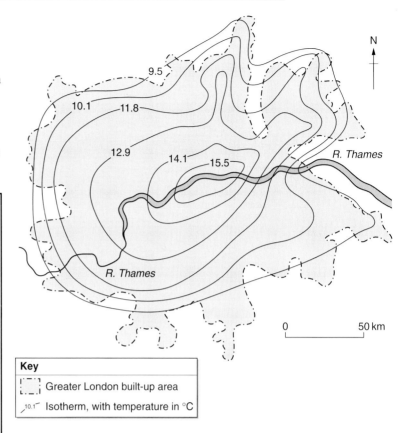

STUDENT ACTIVITY 3.2

1 Suggest possible advantages and disadvantages of the heat island effect for both urban human and wildlife populations.
2 Create your own case study of Greater London's heat island effects, using Figure 3.2.1 and the information provided in the text.
3 The two models in Figure 3.2.3 are often used to investigate land use zone patterns within urban areas. Compare the likely implications of these two patterns for local heat island effects.
4 Describe the temperature and total annual precipitation patterns shown in Figure 3.2.5, then refer to Figure 3.2.4 to suggest reasons for your pattern descriptions.

Key

`|¯-¯|` Greater London built-up area

`₁₀.₁⌐` Isotherm, with temperature in °C

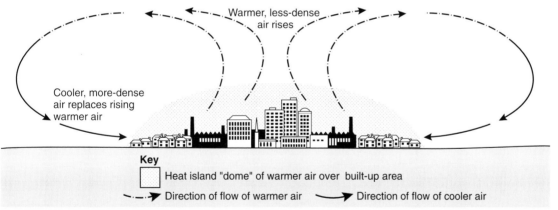

FIGURE 3.2.1 Isotherm pattern in the Greater London area on a typical July evening

FIGURE 3.2.2 'Urban–rural' air flows

FIGURE 3.2.3 Concentric and sector urban land use models

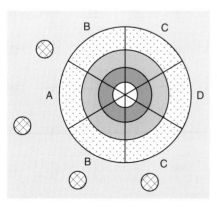

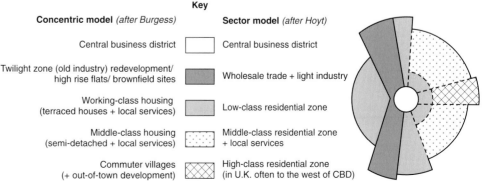

Key

Concentric model *(after Burgess)*

Central business district

Twilight zone (old industry) redevelopment/ high rise flats/ brownfield sites

Working-class housing (terraced houses + local services)

Middle-class housing (semi-detached + local services)

Commuter villages (+ out-of-town development)

Sector model *(after Hoyt)*

Central business district

Wholesale trade + light industry

Low-class residential zone

Middle-class residential zone + local services

High-class residential zone (in U.K. often to the west of CBD)

FIGURE 3.2.4 Urban 'heat
island' factors

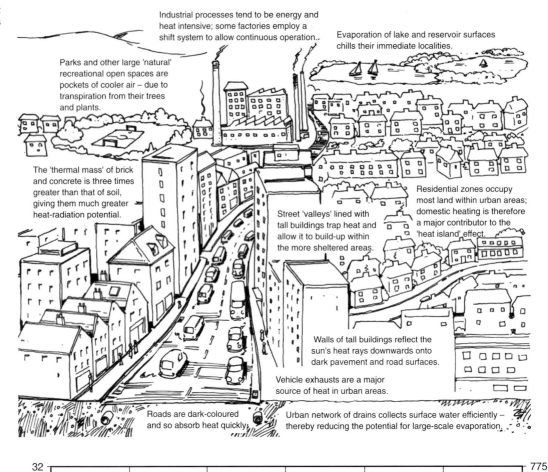

Industrial processes tend to be energy and
heat intensive; some factories employ a
shift system to allow continuous operation.

Evaporation of lake and reservoir surfaces
chills their immediate localities.

Parks and other large 'natural'
recreational open spaces are
pockets of cooler air – due to
transpiration from their trees
and plants.

The 'thermal mass' of brick
and concrete is three times
greater than that of soil,
giving them much greater
heat-radiation potential.

Street 'valleys' lined with
tall buildings trap heat and
allow it to build-up within
the more sheltered areas.

Residential zones occupy
most land within urban areas;
domestic heating is therefore
a major contributor to the
'heat island' effect.

Walls of tall buildings reflect the
sun's heat rays downwards onto
dark pavement and road surfaces.

Vehicle exhausts are a major
source of heat in urban areas.

Roads are dark-coloured
and so absorb heat quickly.

Urban network of drains collects surface water efficiently –
thereby reducing the potential for large-scale evaporation.

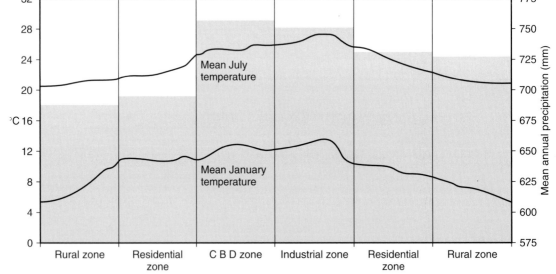

FIGURE 3.2.5 Transect
showing typical
changing rurban
temperature and
precipitation patterns

3.3 Smog

Smog is a general term – used to describe heavily
polluted air in urban areas. In Britain, it is most
often thought of as being the type produced by the
burning of coal in damp air conditions. This is very
different to a more recent form, known as
photochemical smog, which is discussed in unit 3.4.

Air pollution was unknown before the burning

of fuel for heating and cooking purposes and had
little impact on the natural environment until
people organised themselves into settlements for
protection and mutual support. The problems
resulting from increased and often inefficient
burning are well illustrated by studying its effects
on a rapidly expanding London.

	3 December	4–5 December	6 December	7 December
Regional atmospheric state	A 'depression' (low air pressure area) tracking eastwards from Atlantic Ocean to cross British Isles	An 'anticyclone' (high air pressure area) tracks southwards to displace depression over British Isles	Anticyclone over British Isles	Anticyclone static over British Isles
Cloud and precipitation state	Cloudy. Intermittent heavy rainfall	Clouds clear. Occasional showers. Sunny	Clear skies. No precipitation. Sunny	Clear skies. No precipitation. Sunny
Temperature state	Variable, but mild	Falls to 5–8 °C	Falls to 0.5 °C	Falls to −2 °C
Wind state	Breezy	Wind speed reduction	Quite calm	Totally calm
Humidity state	Variable	70%	80%	100%
Consequences		People respond to falling temperatures by lighting coal fires. Air starts to become 'dirty'	More coal fires lit – and kept alight longer. Distinct smell of smoke in air. Small patches of fog form in evening.	Dense fog blankets whole of London. Visibility reduced to only 3 m. Fog turns black in evening. People stay indoors. Widespread illness.

FIGURE 3.3.1 Climatic conditions which resulted in the London Smog of 1952

The first laws against polluting the air over Britain's largest city by burning coal were passed as long ago as 1273. In the reign of Edward I (1272–1307), some local inhabitants were actually tortured and executed for breaking these laws, but even these extreme measures failed to deter people from polluting the air around them. In 1661, John Evelyn recorded that Londoners '... breathe nothing but an impure and thick Mist, accompanied by a fuliginous and filthy vapour which renders them obnoxious to a thousand inconveniences, corrupting the lungs ...' In the 1780s, country folk living as far away as Devon and Cornwall could smell London's polluted air in strong, easterly breezes.

The development of factories, railways and steamships in the nineteenth century – plus the widespread use of coal for domestic heating and industrial power – increased air pollution levels so much that the number of smoke-haze days in London tripled between 1800 and 1900. In 1911 alone, 1100 Londoners died from the effects of breathing smog-laden air, and the authors of an official report on the situation coined the term 'smog' (taken from parts of the words *smoke* and *fog*). Death rates invariably rose steeply during freezing winter fogs, when breathing became increasingly difficult and retching stressed the heart muscles to danger point. Dense smogs in British cities became known as 'pea-soupers' and London-bound travellers would often talk about going up to 'The Smoke'.

Matters came to a head in late 1952, when a set of circumstances (Figure 3.3.1) had combined to produce five consecutive days of smog which was so dense that special protective masks had to be worn out of doors (Figure 3.3.2); visibility was at times reduced to only 30 m. By the end of the fifth day, the city's hospitals were quite unable to cope with their intakes of critically ill cases and the number of deaths recorded during and immediately after the smog exceeded the norm for the two peak smog-months (December and January) by almost 4000. Significantly, the pattern of deaths during that five-day period closely mirrored the changing rates of sulphur dioxide and smoke emissions. The health of many thousands more, particularly the elderly and the already asthmatic, deteriorated both swiftly and permanently. Among the casualties were a number of cows which died while being paraded at London's annual Smithfield Agricultural Show! The primary cause of death in all cases was the inability of the sufferers' air passages to clear themselves of inhaled sulphur-laden fog droplets.

FIGURE 3.3.2 Londoner wearing a protective breathing mask during the 1952 London smog

FIGURE 3.3.3 Chemical processes in smog formation

$$S + O_2 = SO_2$$
Sulphur Oxygen Sulphur Dioxide

(This is the standard 'fossil fuel combustion' formula)

$$SO_2 + H_2O = H^+ + HSO_3^-$$
Sulphur Water Hydrogen Bisulphate
Dioxide droplets ion ion
in air

(Sulphur Dioxide dissolves readily in damp atmospheric conditions)

$$2HSO_3^- + O_2 \rightarrow 2H^+ + 2SO_4^{2-}$$

(Traces of metal contaminants act as catalysts in the conversion of dissolved Sulphur Dioxide to Sulphuric Acid. As Sulphuric Acid has a great affinity for water, the acidic droplets in the air absorb more water, increasing in size as they do so and making the smog progressively more dense).

The events of December 3–8, 1952 proved to be so traumatic – even to a population recently hardened by six years of war – that Parliament resolved to legislate against anything similar ever happening again. The Clean Air Acts passed in 1956 and 1968 created smokeless zones in all major urban areas; they also introduced the widespread use of smokeless fuels and required factories to drastically reduce their smoke emissions. Further legislation demanded even tighter controls on sulphur and lead emissions and much higher chimneys (stacks) were later built to reduce local pollution levels. New factories likely to cause serious air pollution were built down-wind of residential areas and/or as far away from them as possible. The combined effects of these measures were immediate and striking. Central London has enjoyed a 70 per cent increase in sunshine hours since 1958 and many other British cities have been able to report similar long-term benefits.

FIGURE 3.3.4 Comparison of air pollution-related causes of death in urban and rural areas: England and Wales (1951)

Cause of death	Sex	Rural areas	Major urban areas
Bronchitis	M	70	118
	F	47	65
Cancer (of throat, bronchial tubes and lungs)	M	33	60
	F	7	9
Pneumonia	M	45	63
	F	40	54
Respiratory tuberculosis	M	24	44
	F	14	22

These developments have made the 'London experience' a thing of the past in Britain, but similar measures have also proved necessary in the long-industrialised regions of Western Europe and North America. In 1948, for example, 600 of the 1400 inhabitants of the small Pennsylvania town of Donora became seriously ill after inhaling smog; 20 of them subsequently died. The US Congress passed its own Clean Air Acts in 1970 and 1977, requiring individual states to monitor air quality and take action should 'national **ambient** air quality standards' (NAAQSs) fall below specified concentration levels for seven key outdoor pollutants; sulphur dioxide and suspended particulate matter are two of the most important of these and were forced down by 37 per cent and 65 per cent respectively between 1970 and 1995 – even within areas of population growth and major industrial development. The American Clean Air Acts also made it an offence for factories in 'above-specification' areas to take advantage of these pieces of legislation by *polluting-down* to the minimum permitted levels!

In 1989, the weakening Communist grip over Eastern Europe enabled Western journalists to assess, at first hand, the environmental legacy of that region's former isolation. These journalists discovered that air pollution measures do exist in those countries, but that they are flouted so openly and so often that set targets are only achieved for very brief periods – usually when industrial strikes have forced the temporary closure of some of the worst polluters! Moreover it is not unusual for air filtration units in factories to be switched off at night to save electricity! The current pollution situation in Krakow – one of Poland's major pollutant cities, which, like London, is sited in a valley – is typical of Eastern Europe as a whole and is outlined in the article on pages 11 and 12. Coal and lignite are plentiful in Southern Poland but while the better quality, low-sulphur content coal is exported abroad to earn vital foreign currency, huge quantities of the poorer quality coal and lignite are burnt locally to meet industrial and domestic needs. Such burning is often done inefficiently and the air is constantly tainted with a very distinctive, sulphurous smell. As in many primary schools in other former Soviet republics, smog mask practices are a common feature of the lives of young Poles. It is a procedure which they seem destined to continue for many of their adult years.

STUDENT ACTIVITY 3.3

1 Discuss the notorious pre-1960 British smogs with family members or friends who experienced or remember them. Add the information gathered from these interviews to write an enriched account of the 1952 London Smog based on the content of this unit.
2 Summarise the measures taken to reduce smog pollution and quote some evidence of their effectiveness.
3 Use Figures 3.3.1 and 3 to make notes on the processes involved in the creation of smog pollution.
4 Many of the former Communist countries such as Poland still experience serious air pollution problems. Suggest reasons why these Eastern European countries often fail to implement the smog-reduction measures approved by their governments.
5 Comment briefly on the data contained in Figure 3.3.4.

3.4 Photochemical smog

Photochemical smog (PCS) is very different from the particulate type of smog described in Unit 3.3 and is often called 'brown-air smog' because of its distinctive colour. It is a mixture of both **primary pollutants** (chiefly sulphur and nitrogen oxides) and the potentially more damaging **secondary pollutants** such as ozone which form later in the atmosphere when the primary pollutants react with each other in the presence of direct sunlight. As many of the necessary primary pollutants are exhaust emissions created during the combustion of motor vehicle fuels, PCS is very much a feature of the twentieth century and particularly affects those urban areas where traffic concentrations are highest. The equations in Figure 3.4.1 trace the chemical reactions in which sulphur dioxide and nitrogen oxides are involved.

$$CH_4 + 2O_2 + 2NO$$
Methane　　Oxygen　　Nitric Oxide
$$\rightarrow H_2O + HCHO + 2NO_2$$
　　　　Water　　Formaldehyde　　Nitrogen Dioxide

(Vehicle exhaust emissions are oxidised to produce 'aldehydes' such as formaldehyde, which are eye irritants and may also be carcinogens).

$$NO_2 + hv \rightarrow O + NO$$
Nitrogen　　sunlight　　atomic　　Nitric
Dioxide　　　　　　Oxygen　　Oxide

(Nitrogen Dioxide, a brown-coloured gas, then reacts in direct sunlight as shown above).

$$O + O_2 \rightarrow O_3$$
atomic　　molecular　　Ozone
Oxygen　　Oxygen

(Note that the Ozone, which characterises PCS, is the product of interactions between a number of individual pollutants within the atmosphere; it is not emitted directly into the air).

The requirement for strong ultra-violet sunlight normally restricts PCS to the tropical and sub-tropical latitudes – hence its regular occurrence in California, where it was first identified during the early 1940s after the usual smoke abatement techniques failed to produce cleaner air. It is, however, increasingly a feature of much more temperate climate areas such as in south east England where especially warm summers bring still air and cloudless skies.

The **topography** of the local area is also highly significant, as **temperature inversions** produce a reversal of the normal vertical pattern of air layers. The reversed layers concentrate the pollutant gases and trap them close to the land surface (Figure 3.4.2).

PCS may appear 'cleaner' than the more traditional type of smog once so common in British cities, as relatively large particles of soot are not present in it. However, the gases involved in the formation of PCS can adversely affect human and wildlife populations in a number of equally serious ways. People can begin to feel quite lethargic (much lazier than usual) and their eyes may sting for long periods of time; nature's response is for the eyes to water and wash out the irritant substances. Schools may be forced to cancel games lessons and farm animals are at risk from permanent damage as the walls of their bronchial tubes thicken and restrict the flow of air to the lungs. Lesions and discolouring on salad crops such as spinach and celery make them unsaleable; this plant damage appears to be due to combinations of smog gases rather than individual pollutants. Three of the most common gases and their health implications are listed below:

FIGURE 3.4.1 Chemical processes in PCS formation

FIGURE 3.4.2 Inversion layers over Los Angeles, USA

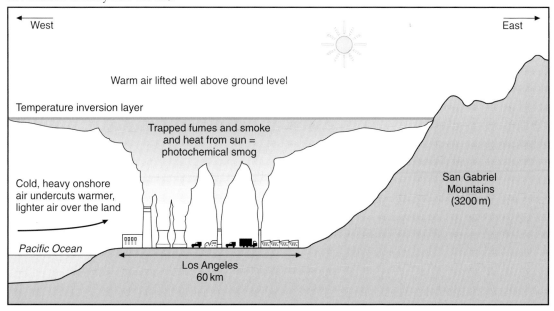

West　　　　　　　　　　　　　　　　　　East

Warm air lifted well above ground level

Temperature inversion layer

Trapped fumes and smoke
and heat from sun =
photochemical smog

San Gabriel
Mountains
(3200 m)

Cold, heavy onshore
air undercuts warmer,
lighter air over the land

Pacific Ocean

Los Angeles
60 km

Nitrogen dioxide causes tightening of the chest, putting asthmatics particularly at risk. Skin irritations may also occur.

Sulphur dioxide increases the risk of bronchitis to the young, the elderly and people who are already experiencing respiratory problems.

Ozone heightens peoples' sensitivity to other allergens e.g. pollens. Coughs, headaches, chest discomfort and eye, nose and throat irritation are common. Strenuous exercise may feel more demanding than usual – even for the physically fit. Ozone and both of the above oxide gases are also major factors in recent global atmospheric change and are therefore discussed more fully later in the book.

The statistics given below highlight some of the issues and trends concerning road traffic in Britain and overseas and the air pollution problems which result from them.

■ Even though traffic congestion has now added 2½ hours per week to drivers' work-related journeys, most motorists would much rather sit in tailbacks than use public transport;
■ Only 7 per cent of car commuters would seriously consider using public instead of personal forms of transport if traffic congestion were to double their journey time between home and work;
■ Congestion costs the economy over £25 billion annually;
■ In Manchester, the Metrolink rapid transit system (Figure 3.4.3) has reduced private car use by 50 per cent in the areas which it serves;
■ Increasing fuel prices seems to have little effect on long-term traffic levels;
■ 90 per cent of all carbon monoxide, 53 per cent of all nitrogen oxides, 46 per cent of all hydrocarbons and 47 per cent of all black smoke are the direct result of road traffic. Particulates come mainly from diesel engines and can penetrate deep into the linings of the lungs;
■ Up to 15 million people could be suffering health problems caused by traffic fumes. Air pollution hastens the death of 24 000 people and triggers a further 24 000 hospital admissions each year. Over 3.5 million Britons now suffer from asthma and the proportion of teenagers experiencing asthma and wheezing illnesses has almost doubled in recent years to 1 in 10;
■ In 1998, the food retail company Waitrose launched a scheme for its employees to place shopping orders and arrange for them to be delivered whilst still at work – thus reducing the need for them to make extra journeys at peak travelling times;
■ Road traffic is predicted to grow by at least 38 per cent over the next 20 years if no effective action to reduce it is taken;
■ Many workers tolerate commuting long distances because job insecurity and their children's education deter them from moving home;

■ The Corporation of London announced outline plans to ban private cars from the 'Square Mile' commercial district. This initiative was prompted by surveys indicating that 70 per cent of all such traffic neither started nor completed its journeys within this congested district of central London;
■ Air pollution in Mexico City is so serious that breathing its air is the equivalent of smoking two full packets of cigarettes every day;
■ The world's annual production of road vehicles is currently 40 million units; the total number of vehicles on the world's roads now exceeds 500 million units;
■ Britain's first public propulsion-battery charging point was established in 1998 – in a car park at Sutton, in south London;
■ The average journey time to work since the 1930s has been more than 30 minutes, but the distance involved has increased from less than 8 km to more than 18 km per day (32 km in the Greater London area);
■ One-eighth of all journeys are less than 1000 m, but many people still use their cars for such short journeys;
■ People who may be prepared to leave their own car at home and travel by public transport almost always choose to drive as soon as they have the use of a company car;
■ On at least one day out of ten, air pollution levels are more than four times above the 'base line' figures recommended for healthy living;
■ Pollution from *individual* vehicles is much lower and continues to decrease. An average 22 per cent reduction in emissions has taken place since catalytic converters were first introduced in the late 1980s (now fitted to over 8 million British cars);
■ In 1994, ground-level ozone concentrations in Britain were discovered to be highest on the south coast of England, which experienced peak levels similar to those occurring more frequently in Los Angeles;
■ The number of 'bad-air days' per year (those exceeding the 1997 government health standard of 50 microgrammes of particles per cubic metre) were 54 in parts of Central London but only 29 in the far west of the Greater London conurbation.

The US Congress passed a series of Clean Air Acts in 1970, 1977 and 1990. These are federal (nationwide) regulations which are then enforced independently by each individual state. These acts required central government's Environmental Protection Agency to establish 'national ambient air quality standards' (NAAQS) for seven key pollutants: suspended particulate matter, sulphur oxides, carbon monoxide, nitrogen oxides, ozone, volatile organic compounds and lead. The Clean Air Acts also supported the principle of 'prevention of significant deterioration', which requires that states whose air is already above NAAQS quality for suspended particulate matter and sulphur dioxide may not permit any reductions down to these minimum tolerance levels.

Congress established a timetable for achieving reductions in the emission of carbon monoxide, hydrocarbons and nitrogen oxides from motor vehicles. This timetable required manufacturers to build cars able to emit six to eight times less pollution than those of the 1960s. The 1990 Act demanded a further reduction in hydrocarbon and nitrogen oxide emissions in new cars by 1994. Even stricter emission controls will become effective by 2003, requiring oil companies to sell cleaner-burning petrol or other fuels within nine cities identified as suffering particularly severe ozone problems. These include Chicago, Los Angeles and New York.

As a direct result of the Clean Air Acts, a 30 per cent reduction in levels of the major pollutants was achieved between 1970 and 1995 – in spite of a 23 per cent population increase. Individual pollutant reductions ranged from lead (−78%) to ground-level ozone (−6%). The result is that, while 90 million Americans still live in areas where at least one of the seven NAAQs is exceeded, 50 million others breathe significantly cleaner air than ever before. However, increased vehicle ownership and an on-going annual increase of 2 per cent in journey distances means that further net improvements will not be achieved without the imposition of progressively more stringent national controls. Between 1970 and 1990, the US spent over $425 billion to comply with clean air regulations. This investment would appear to have been money well spent, as estimates of the human health and ecological benefits combined range between 6 and 33 times greater than the investment involved.

Governmental strategies for further reducing vehicle exhaust emissions are constantly being reviewed. The available technologies are also being refined, but this type of development may work against the interests of the oil companies because it is likely to produce more effective fuel alternatives

and hence declining sales and profits! These companies do, however, continue to invest heavily to achieve more complete combustion by enriching air-fuel mixtures. Doing this allows the hydrocarbons in the petrol to be turned into carbon dioxide (which is safer to breathe) more quickly and more completely. Catalytic converters do the same, but are often deliberately by-passed and so rendered ineffective during the periods when extra acceleration is required, e.g. for overtaking. Moreover, it is very easy to disconnect catalytic converters permanently and it is currently estimated that at least 50 per cent of all cars and small trucks in the United States have been de-converted in this way to improve their acceleration performance!

FIGURE 3.4.3 Manchester Metrolink train

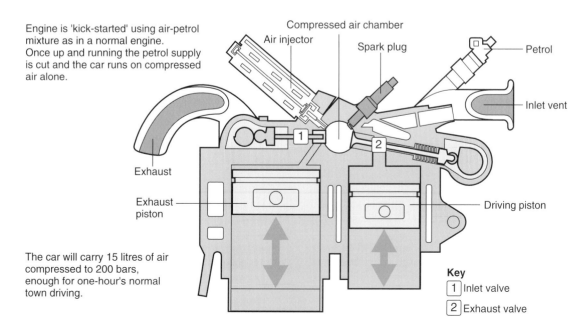

Engine is 'kick-started' using air-petrol mixture as in a normal engine.
Once up and running the petrol supply is cut and the car runs on compressed air alone.

The car will carry 15 litres of air compressed to 200 bars, enough for one-hour's normal town driving.

FIGURE 3.4.4 Guy Negre's compressed-air car engine

Key

1 Inlet valve
2 Exhaust valve

Battery-powered vehicles are now available but their performance cannot compete with traditional ignition-type petrol and diesel engines and their use has tended to be restricted to specialised roles such as domestic milk delivery. Figure 3.4.4 illustrates one novel form of engine of French design which in 1998 began to replace all 87 000 taxis in Mexico City – the world's most air-polluted city. It was chosen for this task because of its quietness and ability to run only on compressed air – after an initial combined petrol-compressed air start. Brazil has been a world-leader in alternative vehicle fuel technology and almost one million of its cars now run on alcohol distilled from its domestic sugar cane crop.

Much can also be done to reduce the pollution created by existing vehicle designs. A telephone 'fume-line' has operated in Britain for some years and may be used by members of the general public wishing to report road users whose exhaust emissions cause offence; each complaint is then discussed with the driver of the offending vehicle, who is required to reduce its emissions to environmentally satisfactory levels within a given period of time. It is a relatively simple matter to carry out exhaust emission tests and the technology to carry out such tests on a column of moving traffic has already been developed successfully within the United States. In 1998, free exhaust emission tests were made available in eight British cities, including Birmingham, Bristol and Glasgow.

There remains the basic problem of how to reduce vehicle *use* and a number of the statements listed on page 38 indicate the difficulty of achieving this goal. The most immediate challenge appears to be to reduce congestion and pollution during the peak 'rush-hour' periods; Figure 3.4.5 illustrates their pattern, which is common to all major settlements. Congestion during these periods may be alleviated to some extent by making public transport more competitive in terms of cost, frequency and locational convenience; safety and journey 'pleasantness' are other important considerations. Park-and-ride schemes now operate successfully in many popular retail and tourist centres such as the historic cathedral city of York.

FIGURE 3.4.5 'Rush-hour' periods for a major settlement whose large area requires long-distance commuting

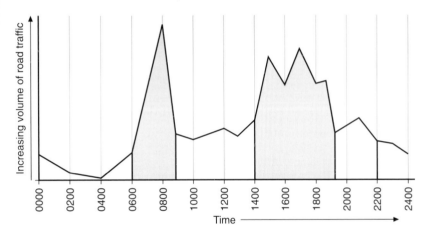

FIGURE 3.4.6 Source: DAILY MAIL, 23 January, 1998

Crackdown on the school-run will cut car snarl-ups

By RAY MASSEY Motoring correspondent

Ministers yesterday pledged a series of tough measures to deter parents from chauffeuring their children to and from school.

With school runs accounting for at least a sixth of vehicles on the road at rush hour periods, they revealed new powers for local councils and an increase in car-taxation.

Parking bans outside school gates will be stepped up, more 20mph zones introduced and extra traffic calming measures, such as road humps, built.

School-run parents are also likely to fall foul of council 'hit squads', which will prosecute drivers whose vehicles are left 'idling' at the roadside.

Seven million pupils go daily to Britain's 32 000 primary and secondary schools with an increasing number arriving by car. Areas with a high proportion of private prep. and senior day schools are seen as congestion hot-spots which can choke large areas of a town in rush hour periods.

Research by market researchers MORI estimates that jams caused by school runs cost Britain the equivalent of £600million a year in lost time – out of the total £10billion cost of congestion.

Unveiling the clampdown yesterday, Transport Minister Baroness Hayman said: 'We need to educate both parents and children about the benefits of leaving the car behind.'

Among measures to be outlined in a forthcoming Government White Paper will be new funding for safer cycle routes and 'imaginative' schemes which get children 'safely onto their bicycles or feet'.

Local authorities could do more to encourage collective travel said the Minister, adding that she was interested in a 'virtual bus' scheme in which parents took turns to walk to school on a set route, picking up children on their way and walking with them to the school gates.

Paul Hemingway of the Association of British Drivers, said the proposals 'smack of the nanny state'.

'Parents are sensible people who would rather not have to make these journeys to school,' he added.

'But when their child's safety is at stake, what is the alternative? How dare they introduce draconian measures which confront parents with the most distressing dilemma?'

Source: *Daily Mail*, 23 January 1998

More flexible working hours are attractive in allowing some commuters to avoid the most congested rush-hour periods, and the trends towards 24-hour and Sunday shopping are likely to make further, if modest, contributions to traffic reduction at peak times. In 1998, the National Westminster Bank took the first major British initiative in this area by inviting its workers to agree to a 'flexi-year' of 1826 hours. School journeys by both staff and students are one of the main components of rush-hour traffic – hardly surprising as the British teaching force alone exceeds 450 000. The newspaper article in Figure 3.4.6 outlines possible strategies for reducing the school journey factor.

3.5 Rurban Zone pollution

Pollution levels are usually much higher in urbanised areas – a direct response to their greater concentrations of residential, industrial and transport functions. Pollution levels within urban areas are often highly variable – as they reflect local land use patterns, climatic conditions and any constraints presented by physical relief. An understanding of the nature of urban development makes it possible to recognise and then explain such pollution patterns.

Whilst every settlement is totally unique – due to its own, highly individual mix of human and natural factors – it is nevertheless possible to make generalisations about settlement development with the use of land-use 'models'. Such models are merely tools to aid understanding, for it is most unusual for real-life examples to reflect their patterns with any high degree of precision. The real value of models lies in their use as yardsticks, against which actual examples may be compared – in part or in whole. Two of the most widely quoted urban land use models are displayed in Figure 3.2.5 on page 30. The **concentric model** is especially simple in concept, for it assumes that:
- the heart of the settlement (its CBD) will lie at, or very close, to its centre;
- the same type of land-use will occur irrespective of the direction from the settlement centre;
- development will proceed at the same rate in all directions. In other words, each 'band' of land-use will have the same width in any direction.

This attractively simple model is reflected, to some degree, in the zone patterns of most of our industrialised urban settlements. It is, however, based on the unrealistic assumption that the land on which a settlement grows has uniform relief (height and shape) in all directions because of the absence of disruptive features such as coastlines, river valleys, marshes and ridges. It also assumes that other (e.g. climatic) factors are similarly uniform – a situation disproved by circumstances in the British Isles, where the prevailing south-westerly winds dictate weather conditions on average during only three out of every four days.

FIGURE 3.5.1 Land use in the Irwell Valley, Greater Manchester

FIGURE 3.5.2 Grime-covered buildings along a typical CBD street

FIGURE 3.5.3 An Industrial Estate on the outskirts of Slough

STUDENT ACTIVITY 3.5

1 Define what is understood by the terms 'urban zone' and 'urban model'.

2 For each of the land-use models shown in Figure 3.3.5:
(a) give the name of its creator
(b) describe the particular zone layout pattern which has given rise to its alternative name
(c) describe any strengths and weaknesses in design which increase or limit its relevance to real-life settlement situations
(d) decide which of the models is likely to be the more dependable in the study of British urban settlements, then briefly state the main reasons for your decision
(e) identify examples of this type of model from evidence contained in the Morecambe and Lancaster Ordnance Survey map extracts on pages 85 and 86. You should do this by selecting parts of both towns as well as considering each town 'as a whole'.

3 Suggest how a knowledge of land-use models may aid our understanding of pollution risks within urban areas.

4 With reference to Figure 3.5.4, and quoting evidence from both of the Ordnance Survey map extracts on pages 85 and 86, describe the range of pollution risks which might be expected to blight rurban fringe areas.

The **sector model** shares many of the features of the concentric model, but also incorporates the tendency for settlements to sprawl (expand) unevenly in different directions. It also acknowledges the key role of major routeways in influencing land use patterns in adjacent, as well as their own, linear zones (Figure 3.5.1).

Each type of urban zone tends to be associated with a particular range of pollution hazards.

■ CBD zones are traffic-congested for much of every working day and their streets, often lined on both sides with high-rise buildings, and act in a similar way to natural valleys in that they trap and then concentrate harmful exhaust gases. Visitors to London often remark on the pollutant-laden air which greets them and the grime which still coats many of the older buildings as they leave a main-line rail terminus (Figure 3.5.2);

■ Residential zones are currently at least risk – certainly in MEDCs such as the United Kingdom, where legislation has forced down levels of locally-generated air pollution very effectively during the last half-century and made the dense fogs described in Unit 3.3 a fading memory in the minds of those old enough to have experienced them;

■ Transportation-dominated corridors continue to generate high levels of pollution, though for changing reasons. Steam-powered trains were major sources of air pollution, and generated noise pollution which nearby people learned to live with because it was of short duration and intermittent rather than continuous – unlike motor vehicle traffic which produces both forms of pollution for long, unbroken periods of time.

■ The nature of urban industrial zones continues to change as heavy industry contracts and becomes more highly localised in out-of-town locations, while electricity-powered 'light' **footloose industries** such as those which manufacture high-tech products are on the increase. Another on-going trend is for new factories and distribution facilities to be clustered together in the form of industrial estates or business/retail parks (Figure 3.5.3). Increasingly, such developments are to be found in what is commonly called the **rural-urban fringe** – the zone where town and country meet. Such areas may be regarded as **zones of transition** – in just the same way that the post-war urban renewal strategies of redevelopment and renovation gave a new lease of life to old, inner residential zones.

Rural-urban (or **rurban**) fringe areas have proved especially attractive to developers because they provide sizeable plots of land which are far less constrained by existing road patterns and compact neighbouring developments than in the more central/much older urban zones. Close proximity to modern ring roads, by-passes and motorway junctions makes rurban fringe areas highly accessible to workers and customer alike and therefore very desirable locations for industrial, retail and recreational developments. Figure 3.5.4 illustrates many common rurban fringe land uses – most of which are significant pollutants of one kind or other.

Green belt issues

The concept of 'green belts', which are able to conserve existing rural areas whilst restricting future urban growth, had gained widespread support well before its formal incorporation in the British Town and Country Planning Act of 1948. The accelerated rate of urban sprawl which took place between the two world wars was the major factor in determining both the timing and the nature of the provisions of this piece of landmark legislation. The prime British example of **urban sprawl** was the Greater London conurbation's doubling of its total built-up area within only two decades of unparalleled suburban growth. Adoption of the more land-intensive detached and semi-detached private housing in preference to the terraces of the previous century and proliferation of publicly-financed council estates were two crucial factors in the high rate of its outward sprawl.

During the 1970s–90s, urban decentralisation involved the migration of retail and industrial functions from their traditional more central locations to rural-urban fringe areas. This greatly added to the pressure on adjacent rural areas, which the green belts were originally intended to reduce! A further aim of the 1948 Act was to counter the tendency for urban sprawl to merge already major neighbouring settlements such as Liverpool and Manchester.

The New Towns Act of 1946 approved the creation of a series of entirely 'new' towns as well as the regulated expansion of existing settlements – both of them largely on **greenfield sites** beyond the green belt zones. These measures provided all our core cities with some means of re-housing their **overspill populations**.

FIGURE 3.5.4 Typical 'rurban fringe' zone

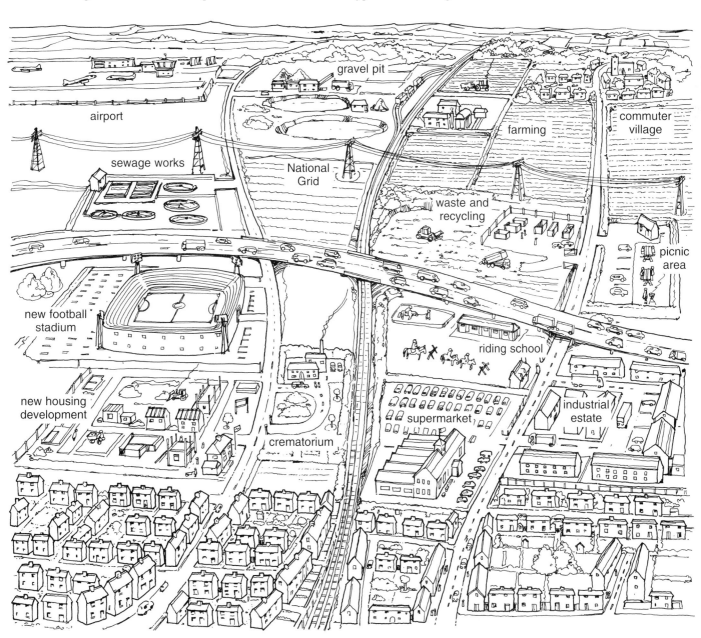

FIGURE 3.5.5 Greater London Green Belt and its associated new towns

FIGURE 3.5.6a Brownfield sites in Britain
FIGURE 3.5.6b Trends in brownfield site availability: Britain

---

STUDENT ACTIVITY 3.6

1 Outline the purposes of and chief reasons for the 1946 and 1948 Acts.

2 Suggest the most likely environmental implications of the failure of the British new towns to be 'self-contained'.

3 Comment on the distribution of available brownfield sites as shown by Figure 3.5.6b – in the light of the fact that new housing demand is weighted heavily towards the south-east of England.

4 Prepare a discussion paper which outlines the possible advantages and disadvantages of revitalising brownfield sites in preference to the development of greenfield locations.

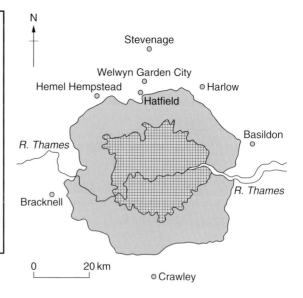

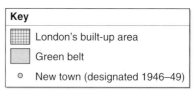

Key

- London's built-up area
- Green belt
- ○ New town (designated 1946–49)

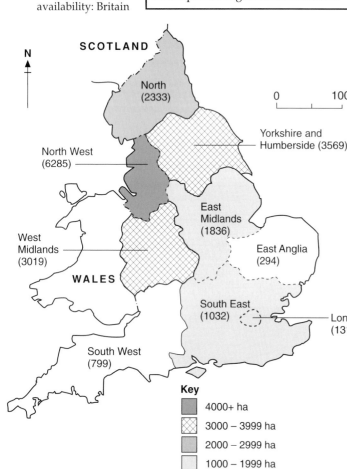

Key

- 4000+ ha
- 3000 – 3999 ha
- 2000 – 2999 ha
- 1000 – 1999 ha
- 0 – 999 ha

(precise areas are given in brackets)

Economic Region	% change in total brownfield site area: 1988–93
East Anglia	+17.2
East Midlands	−19.0
North	−17.0
North West	+21.0
South East	+17.2
(London	+10.0)
South West	+58.0
West Midlands	−13.0
Yorkshire and Humberside	−7.0

Stevenage (Figure 3.5.5) was one of the first of the post-war new towns and, like its contemporaries, was intended to be highly self-sufficient in terms of employment and recreation as well as housing and retail facilities. Subsequent experience has, however, largely discredited this self-sufficiency concept – as increasing proportions of the new towns' 'immigrant' populations have been forced to rely on the core city to meet employment, social and recreational needs.

The late 1990s witnessed the first major developments to seriously undermine the policies enshrined in the 1948 Act. In 1998, government forecasts of the number of new dwellings likely to be required over the following 20 years were revised upwards from 4.4 to 5.5 million; such a residential expansion would increase the 1998 urban percentage of total UK land area from 11 per cent to 12.5 per cent. The biggest planned incursion on green belt land approved at the time of writing this book is for 10 000 new homes to be built on greenfield land on the edge of Stevenage which, if approved, would extend that new town's boundary to within 1.4 km of nearby Hitchin. The ensuing debate has focused attention not only on the scale of the increased requirement for new dwellings but also the alternative option of locating many of them on **brownfield sites** consisting of derelict or vacant land within existing urban zones (Figure 3.5.6). The Government has stated its preference for equal allocations of new houses between greenfield and brownfield sites, but environmental action groups argue strongly in favour of the latter strategy – for obvious reasons!

3.6 Domestic waste

The volume of domestic waste with which every community has to cope is constantly increasing – for a variety of reasons which include those listed below:

■ population growth;
■ increased longevity;
■ mass-production techniques and increasing mechanisation (which reduces the need for and cost of a manufacturer's workforce) combine to allow more goods to be produced, and at a lower cost per unit. This makes goods more readily available and more affordable;
■ recent developments in the packaging of goods have proved to be increasingly material-intensive. Significantly, during the Second World War, the UK's entire packaging industry virtually collapsed;
■ media advertising makes potential buyers more aware of what is available and increases the scope for price competition; repetitive advertising is especially effective in making people 'need' a particular brand or product;
■ rapid-advances in technology mean that many 'in vogue' products such as electronic goods quickly become out-of-date. The purchase-dump cycle continues to shorten for such items and 55 million redundant computers are expected to have been discarded and tipped onto **landfill** sites in the USA by the year 2005;
■ longer holidays, shorter working hours and earlier retirement have opened-up new 'markets' in the recreation and tourism sectors of the economy. As most recreational activities require the purchase of specialised, short-life products, these trends have clear implications for the waste disposal industry;
■ many product categories (especially plastics) degrade very slowly; in effect, they add to the volume of domestic waste which has to be managed over the long term.

Britain currently generates 26 million tonnes of domestic waste in the course of a year; this represents an average of 0.45 of a tonne for each person, and an increase in weight of almost one-third during the last decade. Only 6 per cent of all domestic waste is recycled at the present time, with a further 9 per cent burned in purpose-built incineration plants; the remaining 85 per cent is bulldozed into quarries and other types of landfill site. Such quantities of waste material – much of it biodegradable food remnants – require systematic and safe handling if they are not to become pollutant and a potential health risk. Fly-tipping (the now-illegal dumping of waste on land not set aside for that purpose) used to be very common. Up to the 1960s, the banks of the River Mersey used to be so littered with scrap metal that Liverpool people nick-named it 'The Cast-iron Shore'!

The establishment of municipal waste disposal centres throughout Britain, and the imposition of heavy fines for fly-tipping have, together, heightened the general public's awareness of the need for orderly disposal – as a farmer at Halton, in Lancashire found to his cost in March, 1998! He was fined £7000 for allowing part of his land to be used for the dumping of asbestos and other hazardous waste materials. Lancaster Magistrates Court decided to impose such a heavy penalty because traces of this hazardous waste had **leached** below the surface, then followed the established pattern of sub-field drainage into nearby Gressingham Beck. Further seepage would have allowed the 'leachate' to reach the River Lune – a popular location with local fishermen and canoeists and an important source of drinking water for the towns of central and south Lancashire.

FIGURE 3.6.1 Changing content of British domestic refuse bins: 1950–90

STUDENT ACTIVITY 3.7

1 (a) Explain what is meant by the statement: 'Recent developments in the packaging of goods have proved to be increasingly material-intensive'.
(b) Suggest reasons for the trend referred to in this statement.
(c) Following group discussion, propose a number of realistic strategies by which both the producers and retailers of goods might reverse this trend.
2 Describe and then provide explanations for the changes illustrated by Figure 3.6.1.
3 Suggest a range of ways in which the household of which you are a member might reduce its output of all forms of domestic waste – *by approximately 50%!*

1950s	Category of waste	1990s
1	Cloth and clothing	3
74	Dust, ash and cinders	4
3	Food and garden waste	38
6	Glass items	10
4	Metal items	7
8	Paper and cardboard	25
0	Plastic items	5
4	'Unclassified' items	8

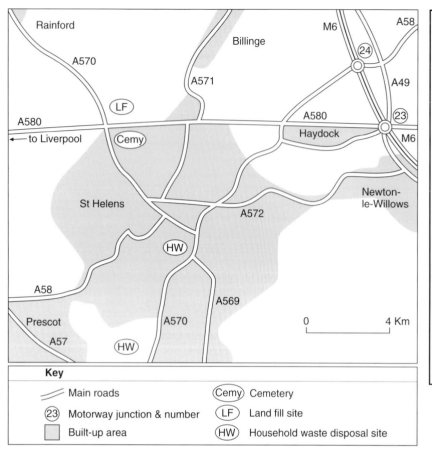

Key

Main roads
(23) Motorway junction & number
☐ Built-up area
(Cemy) Cemetery
(LF) Land fill site
(HW) Household waste disposal site

FIGURE 3.6.3 Location of St Helen's Waste Disposal and Recycling Centre, Merseyside

FIGURE 3.6.2 Source: DAILY MAIL, 10 June, 1998

1 (a) Utilise the information in Figure 3.6.2 to compile a list of the domestic waste strategies adopted by this group of five countries.
(b) Which of these strategies have not yet been introduced to your own area?
2 Investigate the sequence of events which follow the receipt of domestic waste at your local municipal recycling centre. In particular, you should note down the arrangements for waste-separation on arrival and the method(s) and location(s) used for final disposal. Your observations could be recorded in the form of a flow diagram.
3 (a) Describe the location of St. Helen's waste disposal centre relative to the morphology of that town's built-up area (Figure 3.6.3).
(b) Suggest reasons why proposals to site waste disposal/recycling centres and landfill sites are often fiercely contested by local people.
(c) With the help of Figure 3.6.4, describe those geological conditions which are likely to minimise the risk of hazardous waste leaching underground from landfill sites.

How others treat their trash

The world is catching on to the need for recycling, but putting theory into practice is still a hit-and-miss affair.

GERMANY
RECYCLYING is taken very seriously and sloppy rubbish separation of glass, paper, cans and plastics is regarded as anti-social behaviour.

In a number of the country's 16 states, it is also compulsory to separate food waste for compost for extra collection. Germans pay for the service through local taxes and it is sub-contracted out to private firms who collect rubbish on a weekly basis in wheelie bins.

FRANCE
RUBBISH is deposited in wheelie bins put out on the street for collection. In all large towns and cities there is a collection 365 days of the year, but there are no rules on separating recyclable materials.

Certain cities also operate a newspaper recycling scheme using blue-top dustbins kept in the basement of apartment blocks. Collections, sometimes by private firms on behalf of councils, are paid for through local taxes (similar to the old rates system in Britain) but payable by everyone – owner/ occupiers and tenants alike.

ITALY
EACH day, householders take rubbish to the local street collection point.

Normal waste goes into a green container, glass in a blue container and paper in a white container. A year's collection is billed by the finance tax ministry. The average bill is £120 payable in advance. Large households can pay £150 a year.

USA
EVERY city, town and village has its own collecting system.

Trash is packed in dustbins and bags and left at the roadside together with separate coloured containers for recycled rubbish. Glass, metal, plastic, newspapers, corrugated cardboard and aluminium *have* to be recycled.

Collection is mostly paid for with local taxes, but because many areas cannot afford their own sanitation department, residents and businesses organise their own dustbin collecting. This costs about £12 a month for a weekly dustbin pick-up and another £12 a month for recycling bins.

Source: Daily Mail, 10 June 1998

The siting of communal waste disposal and recycling centres is a delicate matter – especially when these are adjacent to a landfill facility. This is because a wide range of often-conflicting location factors have to be taken into account, one of the most common being peoples' understandable reluctance to have such facilities close to their homes. The 'NIMBY' (*not* in *my* back yard) syndrome can operate with spectacular force at such times!

The economic potential for recycling waste materials has been recognised for many years and more than a few enterprising individuals have become self-made millionaires by providing a link between manufacturers and the general public; scrap metals have traditionally comprised the bulk of their trade. Both local and national governments are increasingly aware of the income-generating potential of waste disposal and recycling. In October, 1996, the British government imposed this country's first such levy when it imposed a landfill tax of £7 per tonne. Much of the revenue from this tax may be spent locally – by NGOs such as charities and environmental groups. The government's reasons for imposing such a tax were not, however, totally altruistic! The Department for the Environment knew perfectly well that such a tax would encourage waste collectors and processors alike to recycle a higher proportion of the waste which they receive and compact the remainder before final disposal on a landfill site.

The private, commercial, municipal and charity sectors for waste collection and recycling have become increasingly sophisticated – to the considerable benefit of the environment. Recycling not only conserves natural resources, but is far less energy-intensive than the processing of 'raw materials' for first use. Large and increasing quantities of glass and paper are currently recycled, but there is clearly much potential for further development, as the wide range of performances achieved by the countries listed in Figure 3.6.5 suggests. The UK government's current target for *paper* recycling is 25 per cent, but as yet less than 7 per cent has been achieved.

The following list of statistics provides additional information about the recycling of waste paper:

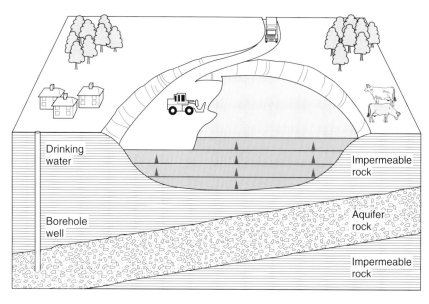

FIGURE 3.6.4
Arrangement of sub-surface layers best able to reduce the risk of leaching of harmful waste from a landfill site

- Japan recycles 90 per cent of all paper used;
- The UK's fourteen daily newspapers alone use 9 million tonnes of paper annually; 53 per cent of their requirements is met by buying recycled paper;
- Devices have been invented which can remove magazine staples very quickly, leaving only the paper to be recycled;
- 140 tonnes of waste paper can be converted into 100 tonnes of re-useable fibre;
- Each tonne of recycled paper saves the felling of 17 trees;
- 90 million trees are felled every year to supply the UK alone with paper and board;
- Recycled paper uses up to 50 per cent less energy to manufacture; it also causes less water pollution;
- Essential fibre is lost every time waste paper is recycled; this means that some input of 'forest wood' is required for every recycling cycle;
- 'Shiny' paper used for colour-supplements and 'glossy' magazines requires a much higher content of forest wood than that used for ordinary newsprint.

STUDENT ACTIVITY 3.9

1 How does the UK's performance of paper and board recycling compare with that of the other countries listed in terms of:
(a) the most recent figures shown in Figure 3.6.5?
(b) the *trends* during the whole period covered by the table?
2 What appear to be chief environmental advantages of recycling paper? Try to add some ideas of your own to the list of points given above; this may involve you in some modest research activity!

Country	% recovery rate for paper and paperboard in:			
	1975	**1980**	**1985**	**1990**
Denmark	28	26	31	35
Finland	29	35	39	41
France	32	37	41	46
Germany	35	33	40	40
Italy	n/a	38	47	47
Netherlands	44	46	50	50
Norway	24	22	21	26
Portugal	41	38	38	39
Spain	n/a	38	57	51
Sweden	30	34	40	43
UK	28	29	27	31

FIGURE 3.6.5 Paper and paperboard recycling figures for selected European countries (1995)

3.7 Noise pollution

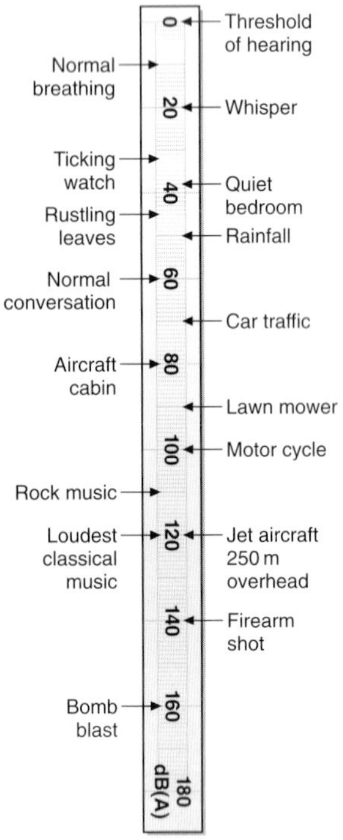

FIGURE 3.7.1 Noise level comparisons – in decibels

Some exposure to sound is essential to good health, as low-level sound backgrounds stimulate our senses; in fact, people who are totally deprived of external sound quickly become distressed. 'Noise' pollution is said to occur when unwanted, disturbing or harmful sounds are encountered. These may take many forms and a low-level but annoyingly repetitive sound may be just as difficult to tolerate as one which is so loud as to cause actual pain. Noise pollution is a quite recent peacetime phenomenon and its origins can be traced to the first period of accelerated technological advance known as the Industrial Revolution (c. 1780–1850 in Britain); developments in manufacturing processes and transport networks at that time led to ever-increasing demands for energy. The combination of all three trends produced noise levels quite unknown before – especially within the more densely-populated, urban areas.

Some of the unpleasant physical and psychological side-effects of prolonged exposure to noise pollution are loss of hearing (similar to that which occurs naturally as part of the ageing process), sleeplessness, severe migraines, stomach ulcers, increased irritability and high blood pressure. Sound becomes damaging at about 75 decibels (dB) and distinctly painful at 120 dB; exposure to 180 dB can prove fatal, as decibels are measured on a logarithmic scale, and a *tenfold* increase in sound pressure therefore occurs with *each* 10-decibel rise.

Increasing numbers of people are in serious danger from noise pollution. It is estimated that over 9 million workers in the USA are currently exposed to potentially hazardous levels of noise and that many more are similarly at risk due to rising levels outside the workplace. Traffic noise is especially widespread, even though people living near to busy roads often believe that they are able to ignore it for most of the time. The noise caused by aircraft passing overhead is much harder to bear because it rises at a predictable rate and the certain knowledge that it will end at an unacceptable level makes it especially difficult to tolerate. Noisy forms of recreation such as rock music are often thought of as safe – simply because people choose to expose themselves to those hazards! Even once-peaceful rural areas are increasingly affected by noise, due to the development of ever larger designs of farm machinery.

Noise pollution is especially harmful because its immediate effects often pass unnoticed. These effects are usually cumulative (i.e. they build-up gradually) and the damage caused often cannot be reversed. The crack of rifle-fire, for example, can produce an instant and permanent total loss of hearing. This is because of the nature of the hair cells inside the ear which translate the mechanical energy of the sound waves into electrical energy recognised as 'sound' by nerve endings. Up to 50 per cent of these hair cells can be destroyed without a noticeable loss of hearing – hence the false sense of security induced by an absence of *perceptible* hearing loss early in the process of hair cell destruction. As the hair cells cannot be replaced, neither can the ability to hear; permanent damage is the inevitable result.

STUDENT ACTIVITY 3.10

1 Justify the statement: 'The effects of serious noise pollution are often irreversible'.
2 Add the implications of 75, 120 and 180 dB to your own copy of Figure 3.7.1.
3 (Following group discussion) recommend a variety of practical ways by which the threat of noise pollution may be reduced. Your discussions should range across all of the following: national and local scales; a variety of human environments; the causes and victims of noise pollution.

CASE STUDY

Manchester International Airport

This case study concerns the building of a second runway at Manchester Airport – by far the UK's busiest airport, after Heathrow and Gatwick in south east England.

The second runway is to be built parallel to the existing one. It will operate only during daytime and normally only for departures, the original runway handling incoming flights. The airport already has its own mainline rail link and it is planned to create an airport extension to the Greater Manchester light rail system, Metrolink.

Environmental considerations were crucial throughout the public inquiry held to consider the planning application for the second runway. The Inquiry lasted 101 days, concluding in March 1995. In his report to the Government the Inquiry Inspector stated that the case for granting planning permission was 'overwhelming', commending the Airport on the range of safeguards proposed to mitigate the environmental and social impacts of the development. Formal Government approval was given to the scheme on 15 January, 1997.

Over 100 legal assurances were made by the Airport as part of its submission to the Inquiry to protect the local communities. Among the guarantees made were:

■ even with a second runway, noise levels, both day and night will be lower than they were in 1992, until 2011;

■ noisy aircraft banned at night, six years ahead of legislation;

■ a 15-year landscape management plan to be established to oversee the effectiveness of the ecological and landscape measures. Twice as many ponds created as lost. Seven times the area of new woodland planted than lost. Over five times the area of new grassland created than lost;

■ works undertaken to upgrade the River Bollin channel to encourage the migration of fish up and down the river;

■ details of the landscape and ecological mitigation works will be submitted for agreement by the local authorities and local wildlife groups;

■ a series of measures to substantially increase the proportion of surface journeys made to the airport by public transport, including:
  safeguarding land to extend the existing rail station;
  development of strategies to promote staff transport services;
  setting limits on the growth of on-site parking;

■ major upgrading of the link roads between the Airport and the M56 motorway.

■ a Community Trust Fund will be established with an annual budget of at least £100,000 per year, to support environmental projects in the local area.

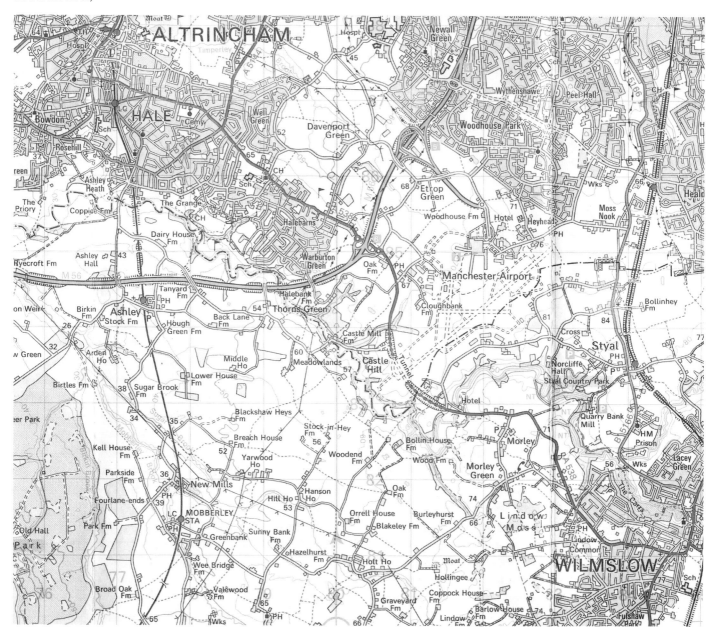

FIGURE 3.7.2 OS Map
Extract 1: Landranger
1:50 000 Sheet 109
(Manchester) © Crown
copyright

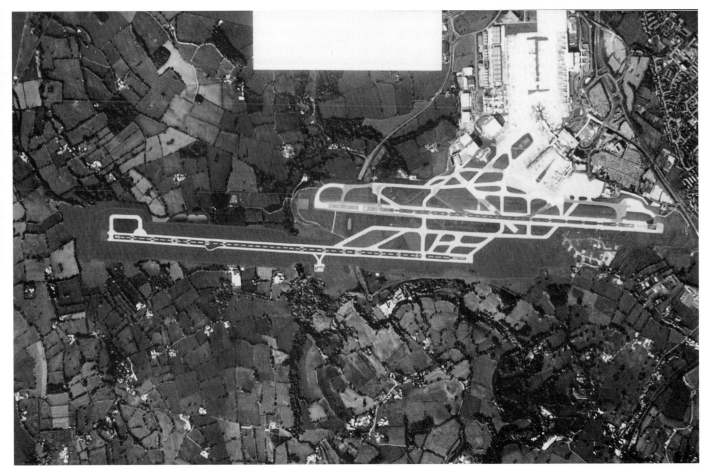

FIGURE 3.7.3 Site of runway at Manchester International Airport

The case for

Manchester Airport, the world's 17th busiest, needs a new 1000 yard runway because aircraft are queuing to take off and land at peak times, *writes David Ward*.

With 169 000 aircraft movements a year and 45 scheduled operations an hour, Manchester handles more traffic than any other single-runway airport in Europe.

Manchester, now serving 175 destinations, is used by 15 million passengers, 95 airlines and 300 tour operators a year. The number of passengers is expected to rise to 22 million by the turn of the century, when the new runway should be complete, and to 30 million by 2005.

This year, 40 new flights a week to nine cities have been announced. Other airlines have already been turned away because landing and take-off slots are not available at the times required and passengers across the North have been denied the opportunity to fly from their local airport.

More than 1 million passengers each year are obliged to start international journeys from London.

The airport has become one of the biggest generators of economic activity in the North-west but spokesmen claim the regional economy would stagnate without Runway 2.

The new runway will create 50,000 new jobs – the employment potential of 10 Nissan plants – according to the authority.

The airport has promised a £17 million environmental mitigation scheme. Six new trees will be planted for every one removed and two ponds dug for each one lost. More than 15 miles of hedges will be planted or restored and new areas of wild flower grassland and woodland will be created.

The case against

The Coalition Against Runway 2 describes the project as 'potentially the most environmentally damaging development in the North-West this century', *writes David Ward*.

Protesters say it will swallow an area of land twice as big as that ruined by the Newbury Bypass. 'The price to be paid by the planet as a whole will be even higher,' says the coalition. 'People need to know that Runway 2 is economic and social madness.'

The scheme would destroy important wildlife habitats, ancient woods and hedgerows in the Bollin Valley. Land in Derbyshire would be scarred through quarrying for in-fill.

The runway would generate more passengers who would come to the airport in more cars which would lead to demands for more roads and an increase in air and noise pollution. The airport would also attract more out-of-town building developments.

More flights to an enlarged airport would increase emissions of global warming gases and destroy more of the ozone layer. The campaign claims the £172 million to be spent on the scheme, including a security bill believed to be at least £4 million, would be better spent on education and jobs.

They dispute the airport's claim that the runway and airport expansion would create 50,000 jobs. There had been no independent study and new jobs were likely to be both low paid and short term.

Source: *Guardian*, 22 May 1997

FIGURE 3.7.4 Source: THE GUARDIAN, 22 May 1997

FIGURE 3.7.5 Source: THE GUARDIAN, 14 July 1997

Rival cities in airport 'truce'

A bold plan to link Manchester and Liverpool Airports under a new operating umbrella will be unveiled today as the first step towards ending years of bitter rivalry between the two cities.

The Deputy Prime Minister, John Prescott, will bring together council leaders and managers from the two airports to hammer home the message that key facilities must complement each other. His initiative comes as work begins today on the £172 million second runway at Manchester. Underground and tree camp protesters, who were evicted at a cost of about £4 million, held up work at the site for several months.

Work, due to begin in the spring, was delayed after protesters built tunnels and tree-houses at camps in the Bollin Valley site.

Government sources have indicated that if the two airports had been working together – instead of fighting each other – the contentious second runway might not have been needed yet. But ministers' hands were tied because the last government approved the project.

Protesters have long claimed that the little-used Liverpool Airport, at Speke, is in a safer location than the Manchester complex on the southern edge of the city, bordering Cheshire countryside.

In revealing a new owner and operator for Liverpool Airport to herald an era of cooperation, Mr Prescott, who heads the Department of the Environment, Transport and the Regions, will today raise the prospect of improved transport links which could lead to a rail link between the airports.

The plan, which could see Liverpool Airport expand into a free port to attract development aid and investment, will be Mr Prescott's first big regional initiative. It will be a test of his public-private partnership proposals, under which government cash should be used to lever private capital for key projects.

He has long complained that the previous governments laissez-faire airport strategy, which pitched Manchester against Liverpool and undermined the interests of the region.

He believes that the public inquiries into the expansion of both airports should have been undertaken in tandem. Instead, the result of the Manchester inquiry, between 1994 and 1995, was announced just before the election. Mr Prescott was left to decide only whether to approve plans for car parking and for freight facilities at Manchester.

The result of the Liverpool inquiry was delayed. Mr Prescott will announce it at today's meeting with council leaders and airport chiefs.

Eventually, trade could be shared between the airports, with Liverpool taking up some slack – particularly on the charter and holiday front, which accounts for more than half of Manchester's traffic – while developing a potentially lucrative freight role.

The sharing concept has long been advocated by second runway protesters in the Manchester Airport Environment Network.

Source: *The Guardian*, 14 July 1997

STUDENT ACTIVITY 3.11

Questions 1–4 are based on the OS map extract on page 45. Your answers to these questions should be based solely on information obtained from this map.

1 Assess the accessibility of the Manchester Airport site, based on existing transport networks.

2 Describe the *situation* (general location) of the airport relative to its neighbouring urban settlements.

3 Contrast the areas which are to the north east and the south west of the runway axis. You should use grid references to indicate feature locations and write your answer under separate theme-headings such as:
- human land uses
- natural/physical features
- environmental characteristics.

4 Aircraft are usually instructed to take off and land *into* the wind as this increases lift and aids flight control at low speeds. The prevailing (dominant) winds over north west England are from the south west. Comment on the implications of these two facts for the internal layout of, and urban settlements close to, Manchester International Airport.

Questions 5 and 6 are based mainly on the information provided by the two newspaper articles in Figures 3.7.4 and 3.7.5:

5 Discuss the *political* factors which appear to have influenced airport provision and development within the Greater Manchester and Merseyside conurbations.

6 Assess the relative strengths of the arguments both in favour of and against the development of a second runway at MIA. You may wish to subdivide your response under section headings such as:
- air traffic volume trends
- environmental factors
- economic issues, including employment implications.

4

WATER POLLUTION — AN INTERNATIONAL ISSUE

4.1 *The hydrosphere*

FIGURE 4.1.2 The hydrological cycle

The hydrosphere is a 'closed' system, which means that the total quantity of water within it cannot change. Much of it is however able to circulate between locations and different types of *reservoir*, ranging in size from vast oceans to the smallest of puddles! Figure 4.1.1 compares the relative total volumes of water's component reservoirs and takes into account its ability to change between liquid, solid and gaseous forms in response to prevailing environmental circumstances such as temperature, wind speed and the composition of any dissolved material. The hydrological cycle (Figure 4.1.2) provides further detail of the flows linking form and location.

Hydrospheric pollution is a theme of increasing concern and many of the processes involved are, as yet, not completely understood. The units within Section 4 highlight examples of some of its major aspects; they also illustrate very clearly the complexity of the task of responding positively to challenges posed by both past and current abuse of hydrospheric ecosystems.

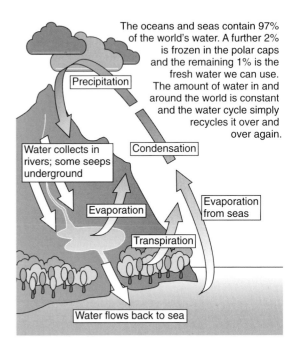

The oceans and seas contain 97% of the world's water. A further 2% is frozen in the polar caps and the remaining 1% is the fresh water we can use. The amount of water in and around the world is constant and the water cycle simply recycles it over and over again.

FIGURE 4.1.1 Components of the Hydrosphere

Hydrosphere component	'Water' volume (millions of cubic kilometres)	Percentage of total volume
Atmosphere	0.013	
Biosphere	0.0006	
Groundwater flow	8.32	
Ice caps and glaciers	29.0	
Lakes	0.16	
Oceans and seas	1350.0	
Rivers	0.04	
Soil moisture	0.066	
Total	1387.5402	

STUDENT ACTIVITY 4.1

1 (a) Add a further column to the table in Figure 4.1.1 so as to include percentage equivalents of all the reservoir totals displayed. You will, of course, need to ensure that your percentages total 100!

(b) Devise a divided bar graph to show the relative volumes of water contained within each of its three component forms; when doing this, consider the 'soil moisture' and 'biosphere' components to be of liquid form.

2 Suggest the possible implications for the water cycle of:
- rising air temperatures
- widespread deforestation
- continuing urbanisation.

4.2 Water suppliers

Human '**quality of life**' is determined by the availability of a range of basic provisions such as clothing, housing, food intake and education. Access to a reliable source of water, safe to use for drinking, cooking and washing is, however, one of the most crucial of these factors. The truth of this is borne out by World Heath Organisation (WHO) estimates that inadequate water and sanitary provision accounts for 80 per cent of all sickness and disease and is the direct cause of about 10 million premature deaths annually. Water provision is a complex issue and may be examined with respect to availability, consumption and quality.

Currently, 93 per cent of people living in the wealthier MEDCs have access to safe water and sanitation, compared with only 69 per cent in LEDCs. Data available to the World Bank suggests that at least 220 million inhabitants of major LEDC cities are without safe drinking water and that many more are forced to obtain supplies from local private vendors at up to 100 times the cost of supplies piped to more fortunate urban areas. Only 29 per cent of the rural populations of LEDCs has access to 'clean' drinking water, compared to approximately 75 per cent of their urban areas.

Considerable variations in official supply provision exist between countries as well as global regions; India's achievement of 77 per cent of the urban population compares very favourably with neighbouring Bangladesh whose equivalent figure is at least three times lower. Global variations in domestic water consumption are just as widespread as those for availability (e.g. domestic water usage per head of population in the UK is over 6 times greater than in India). The purity of domestic water supplies is crucial to a nation's health and is a major factor in determining how energetically and efficiently its workforce can perform. In 1991, 19 per cent of Poland's drinking water was too polluted to drink – even after disinfection!

Inadequacies of domestic water supply provision and quality are the main cause of many of the most common and most dibilitating **pathogens** and have a direct influence on human life expectancy. The following list includes the most serious health hazards which affect populations exposed to unsafe water provision:

■ Diarrhoea, which is spread by the use of contaminated water and/or failing to wash after toileting. At least two million children under the age of five die annually as a direct result of inadequate water and sanitation provision. The annual global death toll from diarrhoea exceeds 10 million;

■ Hookworm, which is spread when eggs in the faeces of an infected person hatch and penetrate the bare feet of uninfected individuals. Hookworms pass eventually into the gut and cause severe bleeding and anaemia;

■ Bilharzia is also transmitted via infected water (Figure 4.2.1). Liver and spleen damage are the inevitable result. Worm infestations undermine an individual's general health and cause chronic lethargy (tiredness and lack of energy). The effects of bilharzia have been so serious in Venezuela that its government calculated that every dollar which it invested in supplying cleaner water paid for itself five times over in terms of increased worker productivity;

■ Typhoid and cholera are transmitted by bacteria. Diarrhoea and severe vomiting are common effects and both often prove fatal if not treated. Cholera also induces de-hydration, causing the sufferer to need constant further intakes of the bacteria-laden water;

■ Dysentery and enteritis are also transmitted by bacteria and exhibit similar symptoms, but are rarely fatal in adults;

■ Trachoma – a disease of the eyes, caused by inadequate washing or washing in impure water. (Figure 4.2.2).

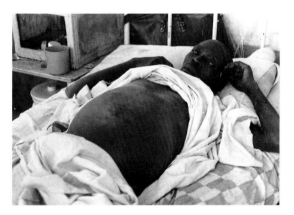

FIGURE 4.2.1 A bilharzia sufferer

FIGURE 4.2.2 The bilharzia cycle

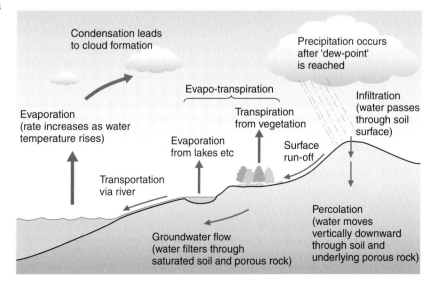

Condensation leads to cloud formation

Precipitation occurs after 'dew-point' is reached

Evapo-transpiration

Evaporation (rate increases as water temperature rises)

Transpiration from vegetation

Infiltration (water passes through soil surface)

Evaporation from lakes etc

Surface run-off

Transportation via river

Groundwater flow (water filters through saturated soil and porous rock)

Percolation (water moves vertically downward through soil and underlying porous rock)

Sources of water

Water supplies may be obtained in a variety of ways and it is quite common for regions to rely on more than one type of supply in response to local climatic and geological conditions. The three main types of water source are:

■ *surface water*, obtained from springs, streams and rivers. The water is then stored in reservoirs as 'raw' water until required for use. As reservoirs are open to the elements, they are exposed to all forms of air pollution – allowing their upper layers to absorb particulate and gaseous material just as readily as buildings blackened and weathered over time in heavily polluted urban areas. Refer to Units 3.3, 3.4 and 5.3 for details of the major forms of air pollution to which surface reservoirs are prone;

■ *groundwater*, occurring naturally in underground aquifers of porous rocks such as chalk and oolitic limestone (Figure 4.2.3) and obtained either by pumping or reliance on hydrostatic pressure which forces the water to the surface. Aquifer reservoirs are immune from direct atmospheric pollution and their water is generally of a greater purity than surface sources. They are, however, highly vulnerable to pollutants which dissolve readily in water and are then able to percolate down to the water-bearing layers. Once polluted, groundwater is very slow to cleanse itself – because sub-surface flows are much slower and so lack the turbulence which would dilute and disperse contaminants. The slowness of aquifers to recover is well illustrated by the experience of Mexico City (whose rapidly growing population now exceeds 15 million) as constant extraction over the last 65 years has actually lowered its land surface by almost 10m! Groundwater also contains much lower concentrations of bacteria, which are able to decompose pollutants; it is much colder, which slows down the chemical process of decomposition.

Non-degradable pollutants often remain trapped for very long periods of time within aquifer systems. The causes and implications of aquifer pollution are discussed in greater detail later in this unit;

■ *seawater*, which may be rendered safe by desalination – an expensive and energy-intensive process – or the more modern alternative of membrane filtration.

It is usually necessary for potable (drinkable) water to be treated by bleaching (to remove discolouration) and disinfection (to neutralise disease-carrying bacteria and certain of the more common viruses). The traditional means of doing this is chlorination. However, research undertaken during the last decade indicates that chlorinated drinking water may trigger cancers and some 7–10 per cent of all cancers in the United States appear likely to have been caused in this way. Ozone and ultraviolet light are safer but much more expensive alternatives and their effectiveness is shorter-lasting.

Water supplies in Bangladesh

Bangladesh is highly reliant on aquifer supplies and provides a classic example of pollution-avoidance which has had unforeseen and quite disastrous effects on the health of many of its inhabitants.

Much of Bangladesh is of very low relief, because it includes the broad, alluvial valley flood plains of the Ganges, the Brahamaputra and many other smaller rivers which then sub-divide into distributaries within their delta area on the coast. These alluvial deposits are crucial to the account which follows.

Bangladesh is a very densely-populated country, heavily reliant on agriculture because of the total absence of fossil fuels and other industrial raw materials. Seventy-four per cent of all Bangladeshis traditionally work in primary occupations – chiefly farming – which involve them in heavy physical work and require them to drink large quantities of water to compensate for sweating in a hot and often 'muggy' climate. Their primary diet is rice, whose cooking process is very water-intensive. It follows that any pollutants in the water supply are likely to have an adverse effect on much of the rural population. Bangladesh is often literally awash with water, due to heavy monsoon rainfall and consequent flooding of its dense network of surface drainage. In spite of this, many of its villages now obtain most of their domestic water supplies from tube wells drilled into underground aquifers.

Until the 1960s, the health of many Bangladeshis was undermined by frequent outbreaks of cholera – caused by pollution directly linked to inadequate sanitation. The response of the international community was to fund the drilling of tube wells, most of them 20–100 m deep, and consisting of steel pipes operated by hand pumps. This aid strategy was based on the belief that deep-drilling would protect the population from surface bacteria.

FIGURE 4.2.3 Cross-section of a typical aquifer

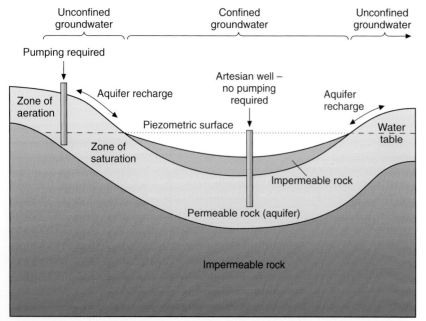

Unfortunately, use of these tube wells led to serious outbreaks of pollution, the chief cause of which has been proved to be arsenic – a substance so deadly that it was the most popular choice of murderers in Victorian times! In dilute form, arsenic causes painful warts to erupt on the surface of the skin; these spread quite quickly over the surface and, in the most extreme cases, cover the entire body (Figure 4.2.4). Bouts of acute conjunctivitis and severe breathing difficulties are other common symptoms of arsenic poisoning. In the later stages, internal and usually fatal cancers are common. Thirty million Bangladeshis are now believed to be in the advanced stages of the condition and it is possible that one-tenth of all the country's adult deaths could be attributed to arsenic poisoning. Recent tests have revealed alarmingly high concentrations of arsenic; water samples taken from 166 wells averaged 30 times the WHO arsenic standard and six were *100 times* the internationally agreed standard of maximum concentration.

The World Bank has stated that at least 43 000 villages which use tube wells are now affected by arsenic poisoning. The task of identifying which wells are safe to use is a formidable one, as it is estimated that one well has been drilled for every four households in the most affected zone (Figure 4.2.5). As many as one million wells could be riddled with arsenic.

Few scientists appear able to agree on a precise explanation for the ongoing epidemic. The answer may be linked to chemical processes which appear to release arsenic from the sediments in the water.

One theory is that much of the arsenic is bound up in pyrite minerals in the alluvium; heavy pumping lowers the water table and allows the penetration of oxygen which then oxidises the pyrites and releases arsenic into the water.

The situation has become so serious that Dhaka Community Hospital now advises local people to abandon their deep wells and turn to surface water supplies or much shallower wells – in other words, revert to the sources which were abandoned a generation ago in an attempt to reduce the risk of cholera! Most of the earlier, shallower wells are now used for the disposal of domestic waste. They could, however, be fitted with sand filters able to remove most of the bacteria which have thrived on the decomposing rubbish. A cheaper, safer and obvious alternative is to 'harvest' the rain which falls on village roofs for nine months in the year. Doing this would utilise one of Bangladesh's few natural resources and almost certainly enhance the quality of life and work-potential of its most important natural resource – its people. Meanwhile, the drilling of deep wells in Bangladesh continues apace.

Groundwater pollution in the United States

During the 1990s, the United States initiated considerable research into the question of 'out-of-sight' pollution of aquifer-based water supplies. It was already common knowledge that the water table level within most of the aquifers within easy access of major urban areas had reduced significantly. This was due to the ease with which aquifer water may be tapped, coupled with its slow rate of natural replacement. These research activities highlighted the following facts:

- 45 per cent of the large public water systems served by groundwater were contaminated with synthetic organic chemicals which pose a potential threat to human life;
- 1 per cent of public water supply wells and 9 per cent of wells providing domestic water to individual households had nitrate levels higher than the federal drinking water standard. This situation was especially common in farming areas due to percolation of nitrates and animal waste;
- Groundwater contamination by 74 different pesticides existed in 30 states within the union. In California alone, pesticides had contaminated the drinking water of over 1 million people;
- In Florida, where 92 per cent of the state's population obtain drinking water from aquifers, over 1000 wells had been closed due to health risks from contamination;
- One-third of the 26 000 industrial-waste ponds and lagoons had no protective liners; of these, over 30 per cent were within 1.5 km of a well providing drinking water;
- Over 1 million underground tanks storing petrol, diesel fuel and toxic solvents were leaking their contents into groundwater supplies.

FIGURE 4.2.4 Skin ulcer caused by arsenic poisoning

FIGURE 4.2.5 Zone of most serious arsenic well pollution, Bangladesh

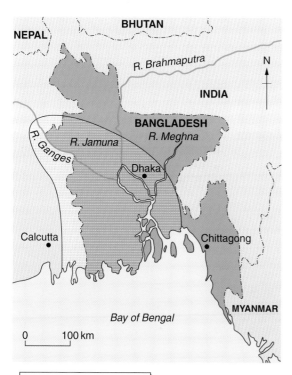

NEPAL
BHUTAN
R. Brahmaputra
N
INDIA
BANGLADESH
R. Jamuna
R. Meghna
R. Ganges
Dhaka
Calcutta
Chittagong
MYANMAR
Bay of Bengal
0   100 km

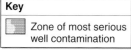

Key

Zone of most serious well contamination

The US government has now taken a range of measures to calm public fears over the safety of aquifer water:
■ All new tanks are required to incorporate a leak detection system;
■ New tanks must be constructed from non-corrosive material such as fibreglass;
■ New tanks holding any one of a list of 700 particularly hazardous chemicals must have overfill and spill-prevention devices; they must also have double walls or concrete vaults to reduce the risk of leakage;
■ Owners of commercial underground tanks must carry liability insurance of at least $1million, to offset future de-contamination costs;
■ Congress has passed legislation placing a national tax on vehicle fuels – to create a $500 million trust fund to pay the cost of cleaning-up leaks from underground tanks.

FIGURE 4.2.6 Sources of aquifer contamination

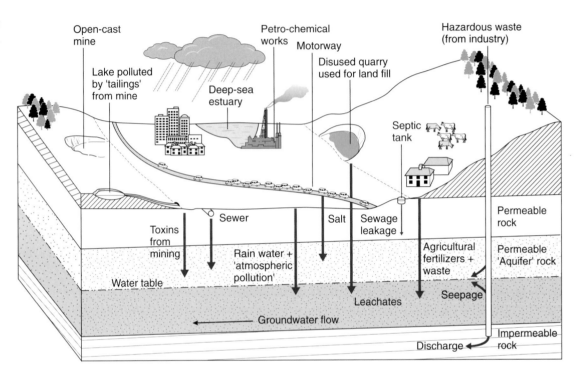

STUDENT ACTIVITY 4.2

1 Outline the range of health hazards associated with contaminated drinking water.
2 Devise a table to display the chief advantages and disadvantages of utilising surface water, groundwater and seawater for domestic supplies.
3 Suggest reasons why Bangladesh may be referred to as 'a country in crisis'.
4 Produce a list of preventative measures designed to minimise the risk of contamination to groundwater aquifers.
5 With the aid of atlas maps providing climatic, population density and geological details of Great Britain, explain why the water table under the Thames Basin has lowered so much during the last 125 years that the piezometric surface of its well has been reduced by 60 m. (*Note: The piezometric surface is the level to which water in wells will rise naturally due to underground pressure within the aquifer*).
6 The safety of an area's drinking water is often closely linked to the adequacy of sewage treatment arrangements. Draw a scatter graph to

Country	Percentage of urban population having access to an effective sewage treatment system	Life expectancy (in years)
Bangladesh	21	56
India	27	60
Indonesia	29	62
Malaysia	100	70
Myanmar	38	57
Nepal	16	54
Pakistan	42	59
Philippines	81	68
South Korea	100	74
Singapore	100	78
Sri Lanka	80	73
Thailand	64	69

establish the strength of any links which may exist between the two sets of data given in the table above.

4.3 River pollution

Rivers have been subjected to every known form of pollution, due to a range of factors which make them especially vulnerable to environmental abuse:
- they are slow-moving and relatively narrow, which reduces their ability to disperse pollution;
- they have always provided attractive sites on which to build settlements, being able to supply them with water for drinking, agricultural and industrial purposes;
- they are a reliable means of obtaining power (initially for milling corn – more recently for generating HEP);
- they offer a convenient means of disposing of urban waste, particularly sewage;

- their valleys have created natural routeways; water-borne transport was by far the most efficient method of moving raw materials and finished products before the invention of railways and tarmac road surfaces;
- they are often used to supply coolant water to electricity generating powers stations; the increased temperature of the used water is a frequent cause of 'thermal pollution', which is hazardous to fish.

This unit examines pollution issues with respect to two contrasting river systems, both of which have been subjected to accidental as well as habitual pollution inputs.

FIGURE 4.3.1 Mersey Estuary

The leakage of oil took place on 19 August, 1989 ... 1250 tonnes of Venezuelan oil escaped from a pipeline in the Mersey Estuary ... the food chain in the estuary could take at least five years to recover ... thousands of migrating birds might starve during the next few winters if substantial numbers of the invertebrates on which they feed are killed off by the oil ... 1900 birds were affected by the spillage, mainly gulls ... 1250 tonnes of Venezuelan crude oil escaped ... the likely cause of the leak was metal fatigue or corrosion in an underground pipeline ... the pipeline carried oil from storage at Tranmere (near Birkenhead) to Shell UK's refinery at Stanlow ... prevailing south westerly winds blew the oil away from the birds' main feeding grounds, which are on the south side of the estuary ... the estuary bottom is made up of sedimentary rather than rocky material ... oil sludge can settle on mud and kill off the crabs and worms that birds feed on ... if the winter is severe, more migrating birds will flock to the Mersey, because it rarely freezes over ... most of the oil came ashore on the Wirral coastline ... workers have mixed up some of the oil with dry sand and dug it up at high tide ... further upstream, boats are being used to skim the residue off the surface ... the use of detergent sprays in the Warrington area was halted to avoid further chemical damage to the environment ... Shell came under attack last night for reacting too slowly to the spillage ... the spillage could impede the work of the Mersey Basin Campaign, in which almost £1 billion has been spent during the last five years to clean-up its rivers and tributaries ... oil was washed ashore as far north as Southport ... in the less accessible areas, workers used only buckets and spades to remove the oil ... Mr. Bob Reid, chairman of Shell UK, confirmed that the company would meet the costs of the clean-up operation and meet any compensation claims ... oil slicks stretched as far as 50 km, from Formby to the river's upper reaches at Warrington ... the texture of the oil made it difficult to disperse with detergents ... the leakage of 150 tonnes was the equivalent of 1000 barrels ... the Shell refinery is alleged to have a history of faults and poor safety procedures ... the company insisted that the pipeline has no history of leaks or corrosion and that it had replaced sections of the pipe only three years earlier because a leakage was feared ... the company admitted leaks of crude oil in two further incidents in the past three years ... many pipeline engineers believe that the Department of the Environment should require the use of a measuring device known as an 'intelligent pig', which uses cameras to assess internal and external corrosion; pigs cost about £250 000 each and Shell has not used them in the Mersey Basin on the grounds that they are too expensive and are not necessary there ... the National Rivers Authority has indicated that it might prosecute the company under the Control of Pollution Act ... the river has not got as good a tidal flush as many others such as the Thames ... its tributaries are quite short and are heavily polluted virtually completely from source to mouth ... even the Rhine has long upper stretches which are virtually pollution-free ... the end of the estuary is very narrow and this limits the ability of the tides to flush it out ... a $40 million scheme at Sandon Dock to intercept and process Liverpool's sewage became operational in the early 1990s and has helped to reduce pollutant inputs ... the river is now being monitored constantly at 20 sampling points using a computerised data system donated by ICI.

The River Mersey

FIGURE 4.3.2 River
Mersey Basin

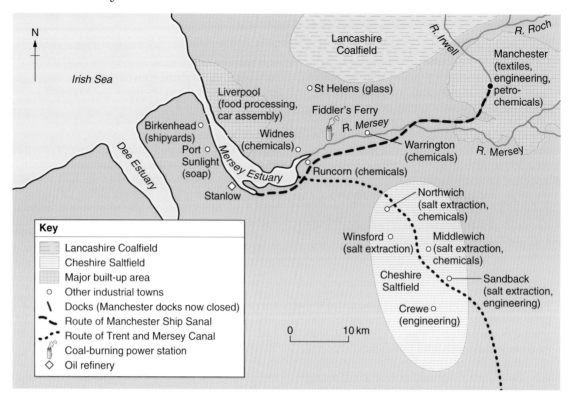

The River Rhine

The basin of the River Rhine includes many of Central Europe's largest urban and industrial concentrations (Figure 4.3.3). This led to the Rhine suffering appalling environmental damage during the nineteenth and twentieth centuries. It is only in the last two decades, however, that effective measures have been taken to improve matters.

On 1 November, 1986 a serious fire broke out in an agro-chemicals storage warehouse belonging to the Sandoz Company at Schweizerhalle, close to Basel, the Rhine's 'head of navigation'. As a result of the firefighting operation which followed, 1300 tonnes of hazardous substances (including 30 tonnes of pesticides and 200 kg of mercury) were washed into the River Rhine. This was the equivalent of an entire year's pollution input.

The effects of the discharge were devastating in the short term. The river was proclaimed to be biologically dead for 300 km (almost 23 per cent of its total length of 1300 km) downstream of the discharge point. Half a million fish and almost the entire stock of eels perished almost immediately; altogether, 34 varieties of fish were seriously affected.

Sandoz excavated and rendered safe 25 000 tonnes of contaminated soil from the devastated warehouse site – thus ensuring that contaminated groundwater could not seep into the river and cause further pollution. The company had little option but to settle over 1100 third-party claims for compensation – a total bill of 42 million Swiss francs (equivalent to £19 million). Further, non-related pollution incidents suggest that other companies took advantage of the situation to off-load their own toxic wastes, secure in the knowledge that the chances of extra discharges being detected and traced back to their sources were almost negligible. In fact, it was later discovered that BASF had released 1100 kg of pesticide into the river later during the same month!

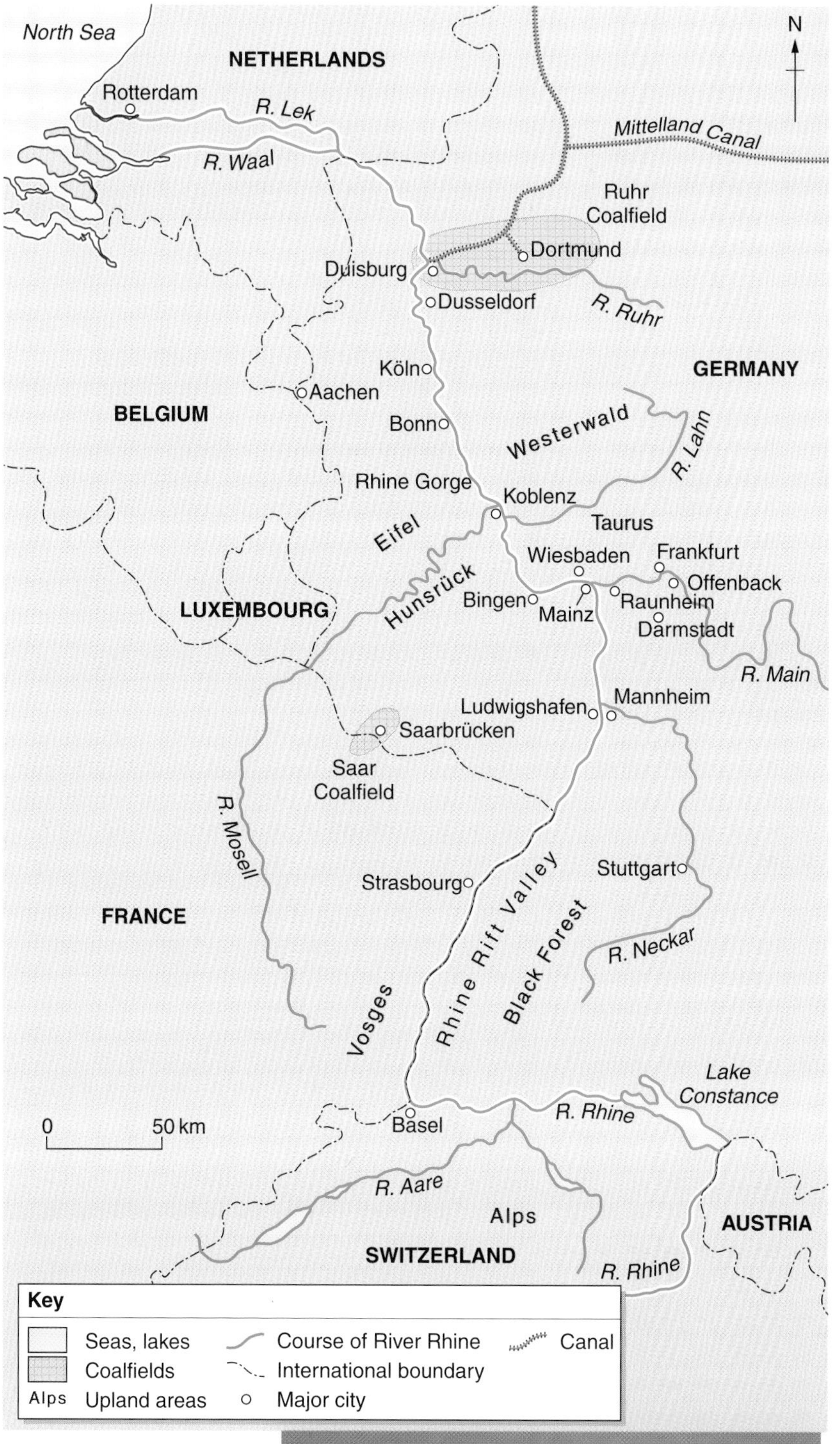

FIGURE 4.3.3a River Rhine Basin

FIGURE 4.3.3b Oblique aerial view of Europort at Rotterdam

N

North Sea

NETHERLANDS

Rotterdam

R. Lek

R. Waal

Mittelland Canal

Ruhr Coalfield

Duisburg

Dortmund

R. Ruhr

Dusseldorf

GERMANY

Köln

Aachen

Bonn

Westerwald

R. Lahn

Rhine Gorge

Koblenz

BELGIUM

Eifel

Taurus

Wiesbaden

Frankfurt

Hunsrück

Bingen

Offenback

LUXEMBOURG

Mainz

Raunheim

Darmstadt

R. Main

Ludwigshafen

Mannheim

Saarbrücken

Saar Coalfield

R. Mosell

Strasbourg

Rhine Rift Valley

Stuttgart

Black Forest

R. Neckar

FRANCE

Vosges

Lake Constance

0   50 km

Basel

R. Rhine

R. Aare

Alps

AUSTRIA

SWITZERLAND

R. Rhine

Key

▢ Seas, lakes	⌇ Course of River Rhine	⌁⌁⌁ Canal
▨ Coalfields	⌐⌐ International boundary	
Alps Upland areas	○ Major city	

FIGURE 4.3.3c Industrial scene in the Ruhr

FIGURE 4.3.3d Oblique aerial view of a densely populated area in the Ruhr

FIGURE 4.3.3e A prosperous farming area next to the Rhine

The average speed of flow of the River Rhine (5 km per hour) proved sufficient to flush the main channel clear of pollutants in a surprisingly short period of time and the main 'plug' of toxic soup entered the North Sea ten days after the incident; its progress had been easy to monitor, as it contained the red dye rhodamine. However, this major incident occurred at a particularly sensitive time because, only six months earlier, major leaks of radioactive material from the Chernobyl nuclear power station had already made environmental pollution a major political issue throughout Western Europe. The responses to the Rhine incident by both the company concerned and the countries most affected were therefore immediate and purposeful.

Sandoz quickly adopted improved storage arrangements which separated the materials in different risk categories and provided special tanks to retain fire-fighting run-off water. These have been adopted by chemical companies throughout the world and are called 'Sandoz basins'! The company had been shocked by the fury of local protestors (some of whom had actually spat upon and thrown dead eels in the faces of the company directors) and created a completely new department with responsibility for accident prevention. The company has now eliminated mercury from its manufacturing processes altogether and a total of 108 of the more hazardous products have been phased out by the company's chemicals and agricultural divisions. Sandoz has funded the appointment of a professor of environmental studies and established the Sandoz Rhine Fund which supports scientific research into the Rhine ecosystem. Sandoz has also associated itself with the International Chamber of Commerce's 'Charter for Sustainable Development'.

Until the 1986 disaster, little was known about the ecology of the Rhine. The river had virtually become an international sewer for much of its navigable length and high levels of pollution had been present for so long that certain species of crustaceans and molluscs had adapted permanently to life in polluted waters; they multiplied quite happily in the intense pollution which followed the Sandoz fire! By 1970, much of the Rhine was effectively biologically dead. Untreated waste had depleted its oxygen content so much that marine life was virtually absent in and downstream of the 700 km German stretch (which was subject to pollution from over 70 per cent of that country's entire industrial base). Contamination near Cologne was so intense that a nearby 18 km stretch of the river was officially designated as a danger zone.

Some attempts to improve the situation had been made as early as 1950, when France, Germany, Luxembourg, the Netherlands and Switzerland had formed the International Commission for the Protection of the Rhine (ICPR). $70 billion was later spent by their governments and some modest improvements in water quality were already being recorded before the Sandoz fire. However, this huge investment was largely cost-*in*effective because each country responded to crises by blaming its neighbours rather than attempting to find common solutions. It was only after the Sandoz fire that scientific research into measures which might prevent future crises became a unifying priority. The fire had provided the stimulus needed for all the ICPR states to begin to work together effectively. In 1987, they approved the Rhine Action Plan, whose chief targets were:

■ to regenerate the Rhine ecosystem so that species of marine life could become re-established; appropriately, a salmon was chosen as the Action Plan's logo;
■ to increase water purity in the river to such a high level that treatment plants could make its water safe to drink at very little extra cost;
■ to establish rigid safety procedures which would reduce the risk of water pollution due to industrial accidents; additional river patrols would make it easier to detect pollution and trace its source;
■ to achieve a reduction in pollution from all sources, including those engaged in agricultural and industrial activities;
■ to target 45 particularly hazardous pollutants and reduce their discharge levels by at least 50 per cent between 1985 and 1995; doing this would also reduce the discharge of pollutants into the North Sea.

Cleaning-up the Rhine Basin had become a continent-wide target at last and an active political issue within the countries most closely involved – especially the Green Party in Germany. Recent statistics show that the new initiatives are proving effective. Lead, mercury and dioxin levels have been cut by 70 per cent while levels of poisonous metals such as chrome and nickel have been halved. Oxygen saturation levels have doubled in some cases, allowing the number of species of river life to rise from only 27 in the early 1970s to just over 100 by 1990. In November, 1995, biologists were overjoyed to discover that tagged salmon and sea trout had successfully migrated from the river estuary to its upper reaches south of Stuttgart in order to spawn there – for the first time in 50 years. However, nitrogen and phosphorous concentrations are still well above acceptable limits – due to the large quantities of fertilisers and pesticides which percolate from farmland within the river's catchment area and about one-third of all nitrogen discharged into the North Sea still originates in the Rhine river system. Rodolphe Grief, the ICPR President, recently summed up the present situation in these words: 'I would say that the Rhine is now out of the emergency ward, but not yet out of the hospital!'

4.4 *The impact of population clustering*

Concentrations and migrations of people invariably have an adverse effect on the marine environment. This unit focuses on the discharge of sewage – with respect to both land-based settlements and maritime trade.

The oceans and salt-water seas comprise 97 per cent of the world's hydrosphere stores. Possibly for this reason, they have traditionally been regarded as the most 'natural' as well as a highly convenient disposal sink. This attitude has no doubt been fostered by the ability of sea currents to dilute, degrade and disperse waste material, but our detailed knowledge of the processes involved is – as yet – far from complete. While careful monitoring following major pollution incidents suggests that marine environments possess a remarkable capacity for self-healing, this knowledge is of little comfort to those regions in which waste inputs exceed the potential for degeneration and dispersal! The growth of the world's population, its tendency to cluster within major urban areas and the attractions of riverside/coastal locations for human settlement are three key factors in the unequal distribution of marine pollution. The following facts speak for themselves:

■ 45 per cent of the global population currently live within major urban areas and this figure continues to rise annually; these areas represent a mere 5 per cent of our planet's total land surface;
■ the number of countries whose urban/rural population ratio exceeds 5:1 is currently at an all-time high, and is also increasing;
■ increased **longevity** leads to a higher proportion of the population surviving beyond retirement age; many older people in the more prosperous countries retire to already heavily-populated coastal locations.

Urban sewage disposal

Sewage discharge into nearby rivers and coastal waters by purpose-built pipelines has been commonplace for many years. Unfortunately, the length of these outfall pipes was usually determined more by cost limitations than the ability of local currents to achieve effective dispersal.

The practice of dumping *raw* (untreated) sewage in this way was the accepted disposal method until the mid-nineteenth century, the only other alternative being to bury it or use it as fertiliser on farmland on the outskirts of towns – which led to it being popularly called 'night soil'. The rapid increase in the growth of towns during the Industrial Revolution created some appalling sanitary conditions and frequent outbreaks of disease were the inevitable result.

The sewage disposal arrangements for the Lancashire coastal resort of Blackpool were typical of that period. The town disposed of its untreated sewage by pumping it through an outfall pipe only 800 m from its world-famous bathing beaches. This pipe disposed of all the sewage created by over 15 million annual visitors – in addition to a local resident population of 255 000 (Figure 4.4.1).

In 1991, a research investigation undertaken by Lancaster University concluded that children who had played in the sea at Blackpool were over five times more at risk of developing symptoms of sewage poisoning than those who stayed on the beach. These symptoms included vomiting, itchy skin, fever, lack of energy and a loss of appetite; unpleasant ear, nose and throat infections were also quite common amongst the bathers included in the study.

In 1992, Blackpool started adding 2000 gallons of bleach annually to its 20 million gallons of sewage – a technique known since 1897 to be effective in killing many of the harmful viruses and bacteria contained in active sewage. In 1993, the European Court of Justice ruled that the Fylde Coast and its neighbouring resort of Southport had consistently failed to meet the European Commission's rigorous Urban Waste Water Directive (which had been introduced in 1975 and allowed member countries up to 10 years in which to conform to the required standards). Also in 1993, the British Government approved the construction of a £150 million water-treatment plant at Fleetwood Marsh, in spite of very strong local opposition! The new plant (Figure 4.4.3) converts waste water into a virtually clear liquid

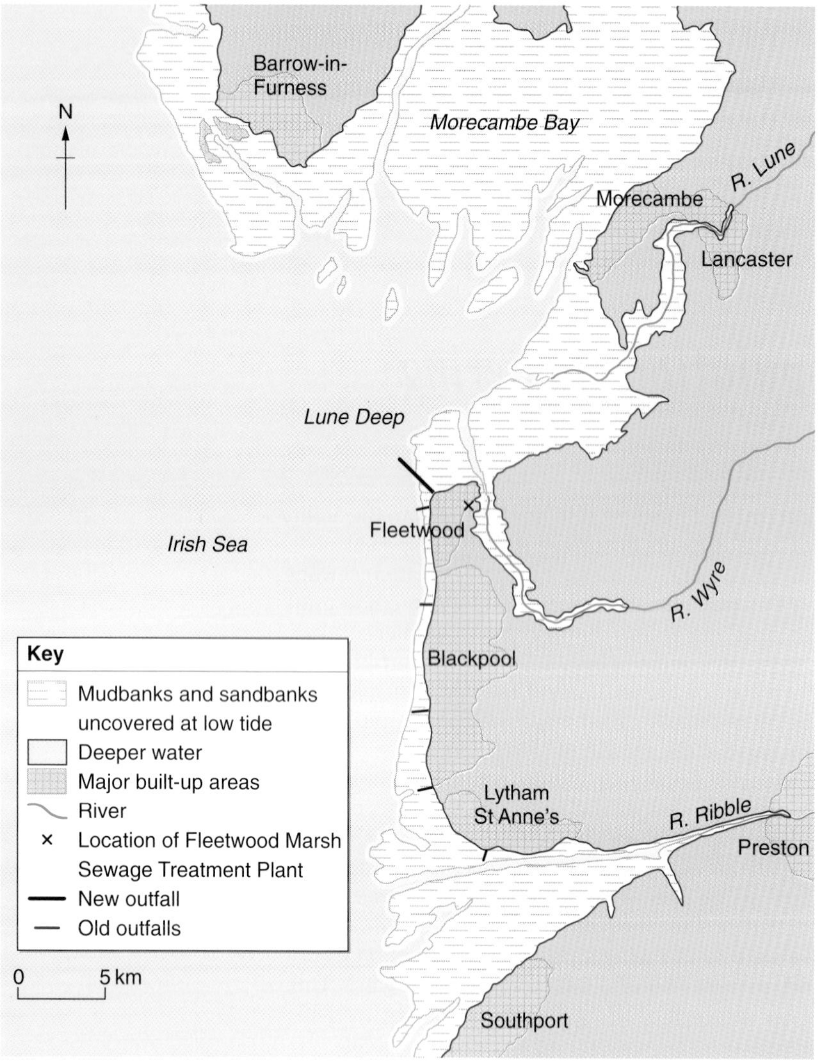
Barrow-in-Furness
N
Morecambe Bay
R. Lune
Morecambe
Lancaster
Lune Deep
Irish Sea
Fleetwood
R. Wyre
Blackpool
Key
Mudbanks and sandbanks uncovered at low tide
Deeper water
Major built-up areas
River
× Location of Fleetwood Marsh Sewage Treatment Plant
New outfall
Old outfalls
0 5 km
Lytham St Anne's
R. Ribble
Preston
Southport

FIGURE 4.4.1 Location of Fleetwood Marsh Sewage Treatment Plant, Lancashire

from which more than 90 per cent of the pollutants have been removed. The treated liquid is then piped 5 km offshore into Lune Deep – the locality's most effective dilution and dispersal point – through one of the longest outfall pipes in Britain.

The latest sewage treatment technologies are costly to implement. The financial burden of such improvements has to be born by local taxpayers and is especially hard on the sparsely-populated but key holiday regions such as South West England, where local water rates are much higher than the national average as a direct result. These improvements are, however, crucial to Britain's lucrative tourist trade, which caters for the 25 million foreign visitors each year who inject £13 billion annually into the national economy.

Beaches which consistently meet stringent environmental regulations may fly distinctive flags to advertise their success. Lists of 'clean' beaches are published annually and the number of qualifying beaches for 1994 represented an increase of 70 per cent over the previous two years. Figure 4.4.3 lists the basic requirements for the two major flag awards currently in use. According to the latest figures presented to the EU in Brussels, 11 per cent of British beaches still fall below the Union's bathing water directives. Beachwatch 97's 2000 volunteers removed 19 tonnes of assorted rubbish from our beaches in just one weekend. Holiday-makers and day-trippers are the chief offenders, being responsible for 35 per cent of all rubbish left on our beaches; shipping accounts for a further 14 per cent. Plastic – the most persistent of all debris material – comprises half of all beach rubbish.

The effectiveness of sewage disposal arrangements abroad varies considerably. About 85

EUROPEAN BLUE FLAG
(Introduced in 1987 to provide comparisons between beaches in all European beaches; administered in the UK by the Tidy Britain Group. Applies to resort beaches only.

SEASIDE AWARD
(Introduced in 1992, to raise environmental standards on UK beaches; administered by the Tidy Britain Group. Separate requirements apply to resort and rural beaches.

The *environmental* beach standard requirements are:

- Complies with the EU's Bathing Water Directive (76/160/EEC)
- Is not affected by oil, industrial or sewage discharges
- Has no 'gross' litter or glass pollution
- Is not affected by accumulation/decay of algal or other vegetation material
- Has local emergency plans for coping with pollution incidents
- Is able to give prompt public warnings if beach becomes polluted or unsafe
- Regular and adequate cleansing of the beach is undertaken
- Undertaken dumping of waste materials is prohibited
- Has adequate toilet facilities and controlled sewage disposal arrangements
- Litter bins are provided in adequate numbers and emptied at least daily
- Dogs are totally banned during the summer season; dog refuse bins provided and notices inform owners that dogs must be kept on leads
- Has public displays of relevant beach information, including bathing water quality figures for at least the previous three years

FIGURE 4.4.2 Beach awards criteria

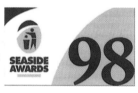

per cent of the sewage from the larger Mediterranean Sea cities is discharged in an untreated state – even though its coastal population rises to 200 million during the height of the tourist season and this sea area is almost completely land-locked and tideless.

In the United States, where half a tonne of sewage is produced annually by every inhabitant, about 35 per cent of all sewage is discharged in a virtually untreated state and scuba divers often report unpleasant experiences close to landfall pipes; harbour bottoms are frequently described by them as being covered by layers of foul slime known locally as 'black mayonnaise'. About 54 per cent of all US sewage sludge is now applied to farmland and forests; the remainder is dumped in conventional landfill sites. Untreated sludge may be applied to areas such as forests, golf courses, lawns, road verges and cemeteries – because these are not used for food production. The American Congress has recently banned the offshore dumping of 'sludge'.

Sewage disposal arrangements in most LEDCs are much less effective. Very few cities in these countries can afford to treat the large quantities of sewage generated by rapidly increasing urban populations boosted by in-migration and high growth rates. The World Bank estimates that 90 per cent of all sewage in such locations is discharged, untreated, into the nearest river or sea. Over 450 million urban residents in LEDCs do not have access to even the most basic toilets and official figures show that two-thirds of all urban populations are not yet provided with adequate

sanitation treatment facilities. In Latin America, 95 per cent of all urban sewage still receives no treatment whatsoever, which places its people at high risk from typhoid and cholera.

Hazards posed by shipping

Shipping poses a range of hazards to the marine environment – apart from those resulting from the major oil tanker spillages discussed in the following unit. Four of the most noteworthy of these hazards are outlined below:
■ tank cleaning has to be carried out periodically so as to prevent a build-up of sludge which could impair the supply of oil fuel to the engines. Carrying out this operation whilst at sea produces

---

STUDENT ACTIVITY 4.6

1 Explain why shipping operations pose a threat to the marine environment – adding some ideas of your own to those contained in this unit.
2 Explain why *any two* of the four sea areas highlighted in Figure 4.4.3 are particularly busy shipping zones.
   Make your own assessment of the likely environmental impact of the 'superships' described in this unit.

---

localised environmental damage similar to that already described in Unit 2.3;
■ crew-members and passengers create waste and sewage in identical amounts to people living on onshore settlements; the larger passenger liners and warships carry over 2000 people and thus rate as thriving village-size communities when considered as pollutant threats;

STUDENT ACTIVITY 4.5

1 Australia and South America provide two 'classic' examples of continental population distribution dominated by coastlines. Use a wide range of atlas maps to answer each part of this question; you should refer to physical and climate maps first, then examine others which provide details of mineral deposits and (in the case of South America) country boundaries.
(a) Comment on the population distribution within *either* Australia *or* South America, then suggest reasons for the pattern just described.
(b) Explain why the population distribution pattern for Western Europe is different from that described in part (a) above.
2 Note down sufficent facts to justify the statement: 'Sewage treatment facilities available to the world's urban populations vary very widely'.
3 Suggest a variety of reasons why residents might wish to oppose the construction of a sewage treatment plant in their locality.
4 With the help of Figures 4.4.1 and 2, make your own assessment of the suitability of Fleetwood Marsh as the site for the Fylde Coast's major sewage treatment plant.

FIGURE 4.4.3 World's major shipping routes

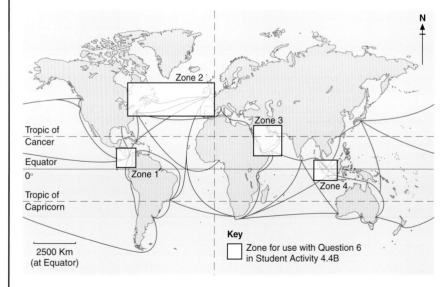

- sailors use the term 'gash' to describe items of solid waste ditched overboard as a result of normal day-to-day living e.g. bottles, cans, food packaging and used cleaning materials. Some gash disintegrates quite quickly but certain forms (especially items made of plastic) are very durable and may pose a threat to wildlife for decades. Some of the more modern ferries operating in busy, restricted waters now retain both their sewage and their gash for disposal in port facilities;
- ship-owners take precautions to protect their vessels against rust damage and the growth of seaweed and barnacles which would slow them down. Anti-corrosion and anti-fouling compounds (e.g. those containing Tributyltinoxide, usually abbreviated to 'TBT') are highly toxic and are specifically designed to kill off marine life around a ship's hull; some have actually been banned for general use as pesticides because they are so powerful!

Figure 4.4.3 shows the world's busiest shipping routes. As most of the routes link densely populated areas, they too display a very uneven pattern of usage on the global scale. Certain stretches of water (e.g. the English Channel) are exceptionally heavily used, while many oceanic areas are not because they do not provide direct inter-continental links.

One recent aspect of maritime trade is the rapid growth in the cruise liner market. The number of passengers carried annually almost doubled (to nine million) during the 1990s. A further innovation is the concept of the 'tax-free super cruise liner', whose sole function will be to spend most of its life underway and ensure that it never remains within a country's territorial waters long enough to commit its passengers to local taxation! The largest vessel so far planned for this 'trade' is the 2 700 000 tonne *FREEDOM SHIP*, expected to enter service in the year 2002. The following statistics give some idea of the extraordinary size and features of this vessel:

- It will be five times heavier than the world's current largest ship – an oil tanker – and 40 times heavier than the *QE2*; it will be 1400 m long and 200 m wide;
- There will be accommodation for 65 000 passengers – in 20 000 units ranging from penthouses costing £3 million each to one-bedroom 'flats' at a mere £100 000 each;
- A fleet of ferries and private yachts will enable passengers to visit major ports which the main boat will have to anchor off; much of the upper deck will be devoted to a 1100 m runway able to handle long-distance aircraft;
- A free tram service will link all its main facilities; these will include a university, a hospital and parks with pools and waterfalls.

FIGURE 4.4.4 *OCEAN CITY*

The Statistics
250,000 tonnes, 386m long, 64m tall, speed 21 knots. Cost £1.2 billion. At sea before the end of 1999

The Rooms
Most of the rooms will be in the three extraordinary, eight-storey hotel blocks. Many will have balconies

The Extras
Six swimming pools, half-mile jogging track, 2,000-seat Broadway theatre – and helicopter pad

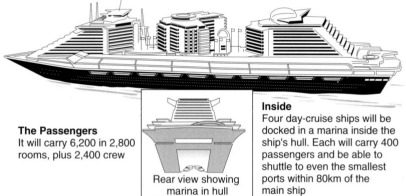

The Passengers
It will carry 6,200 in 2,800 rooms, plus 2,400 crew

Rear view showing marina in hull

Inside
Four day-cruise ships will be docked in a marina inside the ship's hull. Each will carry 400 passengers and be able to shuttle to even the smallest ports within 80km of the main ship

4.5 Oil tanker spillages

FIGURE 4.5.1 World's largest oil tankers: 1890–1995

Year	Tonnage of the world's largest tanker in that year
1890	5000
1910	9000
1930	22 000
1950	28 000
1960	70 000
1966	165 000
1968	210 000
1977	365 000
1985	564 739
1995	564 763

A large ship in distress is one of the most dramatic scenes it is possible to witness. The development of supertankers – some capable of carrying hundreds of thousands of tonnes of **crude oil** between oilfield and **refinery** – has added a major environmental dimension to such events, which was previously experienced only during the two World Wars. Figure 4.5.1 traces the progressive growth of tanker size during the last century. While increasing size was largely a response to market forces such as **economy of scale**, historical events have also proved very influential at certain times.

Major pollution incidents involving oil tankers have provoked such widespread concern that some of the ships involved have become familiar household names. Some notable examples are listed in Figure 4.5.3.

STUDENT ACTIVITY 4.7

1 (a) Plot the information in Figure 4.5.1 in the form of a line graph.

(b) Use your completed graph to describe how maximum tanker size changed at varying rates between 1890 and 1995.

(c) Suggest reasons for the *variable* trend in size increase which you have just described – under the following headings:
- changing demands for oil-based products
- the principle of 'economy of scale', as applied to ships of different sizes
- the impact of historical events, such as the two World Wars and the enforced re-routing of tankers around southern Africa following the closures of the Suez Canal during the 1950s and 1960s.

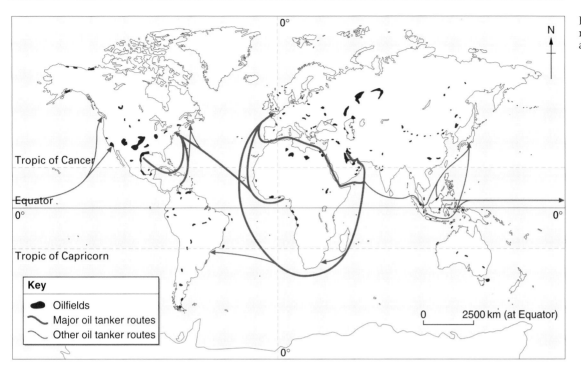

Figure 4.5.2 World's major oilfield locations and tanker routes

Key
- Oilfields
- Major oil tanker routes
- Other oil tanker routes

0   2500 km (at Equator)

Year of incident	Incident location	Name of ship	Cause of incident	Oil lost (in tonnes)
1967	Cornwall, England	TORREY CANYON	grounding	33 000
1976	La Coruña, Spain	URQUILOA	grounding	100 000
1977	North Pacific Ocean	KAWAIIAN PRINCE	fire	99 000
1979	Trinidad, West Indies	ATLANTIC EXPRESS and AEGEAN CAPTAIN	collision	300 000
1987	Brittany, France	AMOCO CADIZ	grounding	60 000
1989	Alaska, N. America	EXXON VALDEZ	grounding	42 000
1993	Shetland, Scotland	BRAER	grounding	85 000
1996	Milford Haven, Wales	SEA EMPRESS	grounding	71 800
1997	Tokyo, Japan	DIAMOND GRACE	grounding	13 400

Figure 4.5.3 Major oil tanker spillages: 1967–98

CASE STUDY

The SEA EMPRESS disaster

This case study is based on the *SEA EMPRESS*, which ran aground at the entrance to Milford Haven deep-water oil terminal, in South West Wales, during February, 1996.

The Ship *SEA EMPRESS* is a standard, 'single-hulled' tanker with a draft (underwater depth) of 22 m when fully loaded. Her owners and builders had just escaped a European Union ruling requiring all new ships carrying dangerous cargoes such as crude oil to be double-hulled, with a minimum of 2 m buffer-space between the inner and outer layers of hull plating. The *SEA EMPRESS* was built in Spain and had recently been certified as seaworthy. At the time of her grounding, *SEA EMPRESS* was sailing between Scotland and Wales with a cargo of 130 018 tonnes of light crude oil owned by the multinational company Texaco. The oil had been extracted from the Forties Oilfield in the North Sea and was being taken to Milford Haven to be refined.

The Location Milford Haven is an ideal location for a deepwater port handling very large crude carriers or VLCCs. South West Wales possesses one of Britain's richest marine habitats: the 34 km long haven supports over 7000 waders and other wildfowl; the offshore islands of Skomer and Skokholm provide breeding grounds for huge sea bird colonies; the seabed around Skomer, where grey seals and bottle-nosed dolphins thrive, is the only *marine* nature reserve area in Wales. West Wales is an important tourist area, with over £200 million generated annually by visiting tourists. Fishing is Pembrokeshire's second most important local industry and injects over £7 million each year into the regional economy – largely through the 500 people employed as boat crews. Crab and lobster catches alone are worth £1.5 million and the nearby Carmarthen Bay seabed's banks produce exports of cockles, muscles and whelks to Japan and Korea (where they are regarded as powerful aphrodisiacs and may fetch as much as £500 a tonne). Any sudden cancellation of such export orders could trigger damaging overseas compensation claims for lost business.

The Incident The ship ran aground for the first time on Thursday, 15 February, 1996 but was re-floated by four tugs early the following morning and anchored in deeper water. She lost about 1000 tonnes of oil during that first day. The weather began to deteriorate at about noon and, on the Saturday afternoon, seven tugs turned the ship round so that her bows would face the expected storm from seaward; she later ran aground off St. Anne's Head (Figure 4.5.4) but re-floated and grounded again a number of times between Sunday and Tuesday, when wind speeds reached gale force and sometimes exceeded 110 km per hour. She floated free for the last time at 1800 on the Wednesday and was then berthed alongside Herbrandston Jetty, in Milford Haven, having lost a total of 71 800 tonnes of crude oil during the course of her seven-day ordeal. *SEA EMPRESS* was later towed to a Belfast shipyard, where she was repaired and made fit for further active service.

The Findings of the Official Enquiry into the Incident (published in March, 1997)
1 The ship was found to be fit for sea in every respect. It was, however, predicted that oil pollution from the initial grounding would have been unlikely had she been fitted with a double-hull (a long-term international aim following the *EXXON VALDEZ* and other similar incidents).
2 All the organisations, companies and individuals concerned were judged to have responded promptly to assist the casualty.
3 All orders given to move the casualty after the initial grounding were believed to be correct; the decisions not to beach her or take her further out to sea were also supported. However, it was considered surprising that the possibility of lightening her load and taking her into port much earlier had not been more thoroughly investigated.
4 *The primary cause of the initial grounding was judged to be pilot error.* The training arrangements for the pilots of large tankers were considered inadequate. National minimum standards of pilot training should be introduced, similar to those which already exist for ships' officers. The standard of pilot training at Milford Haven was unsatisfactory and in need of urgent review. Consideration should be given to the use of simulators for the training and examination of

FIGURE 4.5.4 *SEA EMPRESS* aground, St. Anne's Head, South Wales

pilots. There were poor working relationships between Milford Haven Port Authority and its pilots which threatened the safe operation of the port; during the course of the Enquiry's investigation, the pilots accused the port authority of being more concerned with cost-cutting than improving safety standards!
5 The pilot had not discussed and agreed his pilotage passage plan with the Master of the *SEA EMPRESS* before entering harbour; this meant that neither the Master nor his Chief Officer could recognise that the pilot's changes of course were too small to counter the effect of the tidal stream on the ship's course. In this respect, the Master had failed to comply with his own company's orders. Such discussions between the pilot and a ship's officers should be made compulsory.
6 Lack of knowledge of local tidal stream patterns was found to be a major factor in both the initial and the subsequent groundings; a new study of these patterns was recommended.
7 Whilst the poor operational state of the port's radar equipment did not actually contribute to the incident, its erratic performance since October 1995 was totally unacceptable.
8 The use of an 'escort' tug would not have avoided the initial grounding, but might have avoided the later groundings; further consideration should be given to the deployment of an escort tug at Milford Haven. Two large Coastguard Agency tugs were available at the time of the incident and should have been diverted to Milford Haven soon after the initial grounding.
9 The onshore management team became too large and unwieldy to cope with a rapidly-changing salvage incident; the team did not have a clear,

authoritative leader and communications between the management and salvage teams were poor. Key personnel of the Marine Pollution Control Unit (MPCV) ashore should not have been diverted from their primary tasks to brief the media at important stages of the salvage operation. The unit did not include enough salvage experts to carry out all the demands placed upon it. On the Tuesday night, it was unclear whether the Government was going to exercise its Intervention Powers (authorised by Parliament under the Merchant Shipping Act) to assume direct responsibility for the salvage operation; this caused confusion and uncertainty amongst the local 'command and control' team. The UK National Contingency Plan for marine accidents and pollution incidents should make it absolutely clear when tactical control needs to be transferred to a higher authority.

10   There should be a review of local Marine Pollution Control Units' powers to charter ships, aircraft and equipment quickly in the event of a pollution incident; the existence of pre-drafted outline commercial agreements would speed-up the chartering process considerably.

FIGURE 4.5.5 Impact of the *SEA EMPRESS* oil spillage on the Pembrokeshire Coast

Flora and fauna affected include:-

Birds	6,900 (covering 28 species) were oiled. Of these 66% were Scoter and 28% Razor Bills or Guillemots.
Shellfish	Limpets were heavily affected with average 50% mortality but reaching 90% in one colony. So too were Periwinkles and Barnacles. 80% of a rare Cushion Starfish colony in West Angle Bay were wiped out.
Marine vegetation	Colonies of rare narrow-leaved eelgrass were damaged.
Mammals	Although no deaths were directly attributable to the spillage, 35 seals were recovered badly oiled and other mammals (e.g. Dolphins) were affected by damage to food chain.
Amphibians	Similarly, species such as Leatherback Turtles were affected by damage to food chain.

Toxic chemicals are expected to continue to affect the area for up to 10 years.

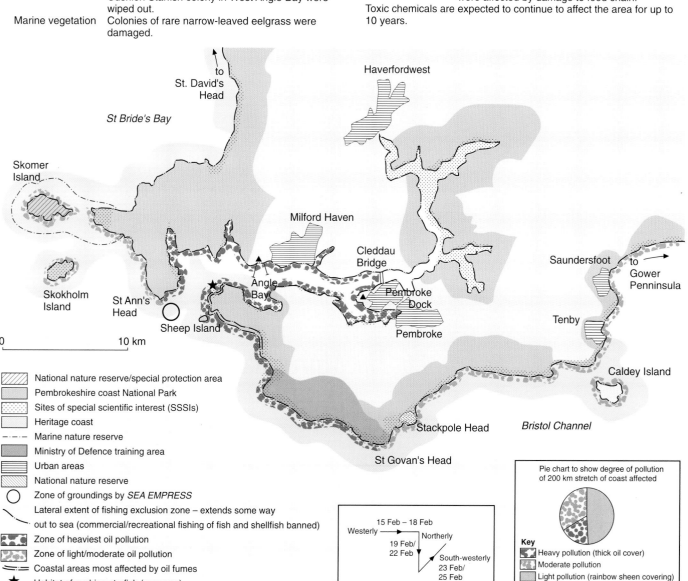

FIGURE 4.5.6 Maritime oil pollution control methods

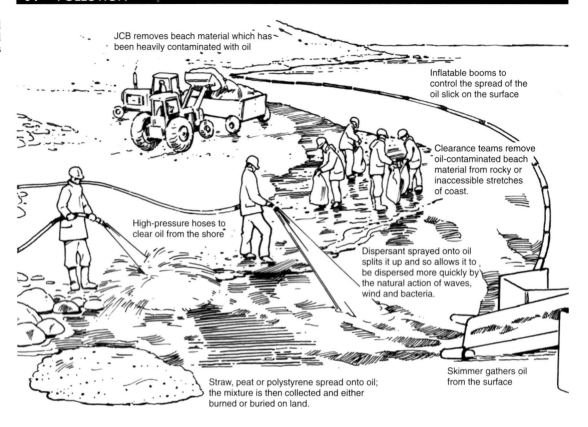

JCB removes beach material which has been heavily contaminated with oil

Inflatable booms to control the spread of the oil slick on the surface

Clearance teams remove oil-contaminated beach material from rocky or inaccessible stretches of coast.

High-pressure hoses to clear oil from the shore

Dispersant sprayed onto oil splits it up and so allows it to be dispersed more quickly by the natural action of waves, wind and bacteria.

Skimmer gathers oil from the surface

Straw, peat or polystyrene spread onto oil; the mixture is then collected and either burned or buried on land.

STUDENT ACTIVITY 4.9

1 Outline the main reasons for the initial grounding of the *SEA EMPRESS*. You are recommended to group together factors of a similar nature, under separate theme-headings such as:
- natural causes;
- organisational and administrative failures;
- failure on the part of individuals;
- lack of financial investment.

2 List the conflicting issues surrounding large-scale and environmentally-sensitive developments such as the Milford Haven oil refineries in South West Wales.

3 With the help of Figure 4.5.6, describe the methods available to the *SEA EMPRESS* pollution control teams. Suggest reasons why some of these control measures might have proved ineffective in view of the prevailing weather and sea conditions.

4 With reference to Figure 4.5.5, summarise the environmental consequences of the *SEA EMPRESS* incident.

4.6 *The Marine cocktail effect*

During the early summer of 1988, two apparently isolated incidents suddenly heightened public interest in the environmental state of the North Sea:
- In April, a well-established seal colony off the Danish island of Anholt lost almost one hundred of its pups through premature births; sickness in many of its adult seals also resulted in a number of fatalities – a pattern which was repeated firstly along the Danish and Swedish coasts of the Kategatt and then as far west as Britain. Eventually, over half of the total North Sea seal population became affected in some way or other and the final death toll exceeded 16 000. The outbreak was due to the

spread of a virus related to canine distemper, later attributed to PCBs and other pollutant chemicals able to suppress the seals' natural immunity systems against disease.
- On 9 May, the owner of a rainbow trout farm near Gothenburg (on the west coast of Sweden) noted that his fish were becoming increasingly distressed. He also noticed that this coincided with a yellow discolouration of the sea water in that area. During the next three weeks, this soup-like algal bloom of microscopic single-celled plants grew very rapidly, at one stage by over 50 km in a single day, and drifted north westwards along the Swedish and

Norwegian coasts. When it reached its maximum size, its total length exceeded 1000 km. The algae released a lethal toxin which disrupted the nervous system and caused the deaths of some 600 tonnes of caged salmon and trout at several fish farms in the course of its path. As the bloom was concentrated in the surface layers of water, most wild shoals of adult cod and herring were, however, able to escape unharmed, but the younger and therefore weaker fish perished in large numbers. Seaweed, lobsters and crab were also affected and caused serious financial hardship to many communities dependent upon them for their livelihood. The floating pens were towed away from the dangerous coastal waters to the relative safety of the Norwegian fjords – a delicate operation, as the fish inside had to swim at the towing speed and be rested at intervals to avoid them becoming exhausted. The bloom of Chrysochromulina algae was later attributed to eutrophication caused by over-enrichment of the sea by nutrients – at the time of year when increasing sunlight and higher water temperatures would encourage the bloom's growth.

At the time, it was assumed that decades of discharging sewage and other effluents was the primary cause of both of these incidents. However, intensive monitoring of pollutant inputs into North Sea waters (Figure 4.6.1) shows that the input pattern is much more complicated than was first thought.

The development of many densely-populated, industrial regions along both its coasts and many feeder-rivers has led to the North Sea becoming one of the world's 'richest' pollutant sinks. Although only a modest marine area in global terms, it is subject to quite complex patterns of sea currents; these currents combine with seasonal and more frequent shifts in wind direction to ensure that any pollution of its waters quickly becomes a matter of international concern (Figure 4.6.3). This map, and the newspaper article in Figure 4.6.4 (which represents a somewhat cynical view of the situation in the early 1990s!), illustrate very clearly the scale of the task facing the North Sea states – those countries who share both the responsibility for and the effects of the pollution which they create.

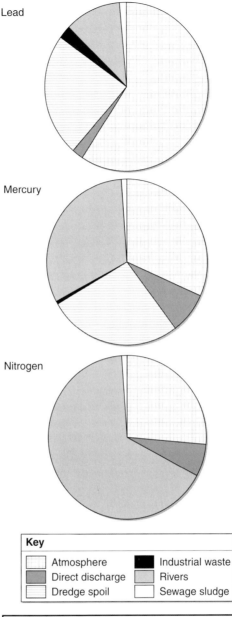

FIGURE 4.6.1 North Sea: pollution input sources

Key

Atmosphere	Industrial waste
Direct discharge	Rivers
Dredge spoil	Sewage sludge

FIGURE 4.6.2 Key data on the North Sea

NORTH SEA FACT-FILE

Area of water: 750 000 square kilometres.

Volume of water: 94 000 cubic kilometres.

Deepest point: 700 m (in Norwegian Trench – due to erosion by Scandinavian ice sheets). Average depth in northern part is 150 m.

Shallowest point: 15 m (over Dogger Bank – caused by deposition of terminal moraine linking East Anglia and central Denmark at the end of the Ice Age). Average depth in southern part is 25 m.

Water circulation pattern: generally anti-clockwise.

Maximum tidal range: 11 m (high by global standards).

'Self-flushing' period: 4 years

Under-lying rock type: sedimentary – deposited over the previous 250 million years. Many of its porous rock layers form 'traps' containing oil (mainly in the north) and natural gas (mainly in the south).

Combined catchment areas of contributory rivers: 850 000 sq.km.

Combined population of adjacent countries: 248 million

FIGURE 4.6.3 North Sea:
environmental factors

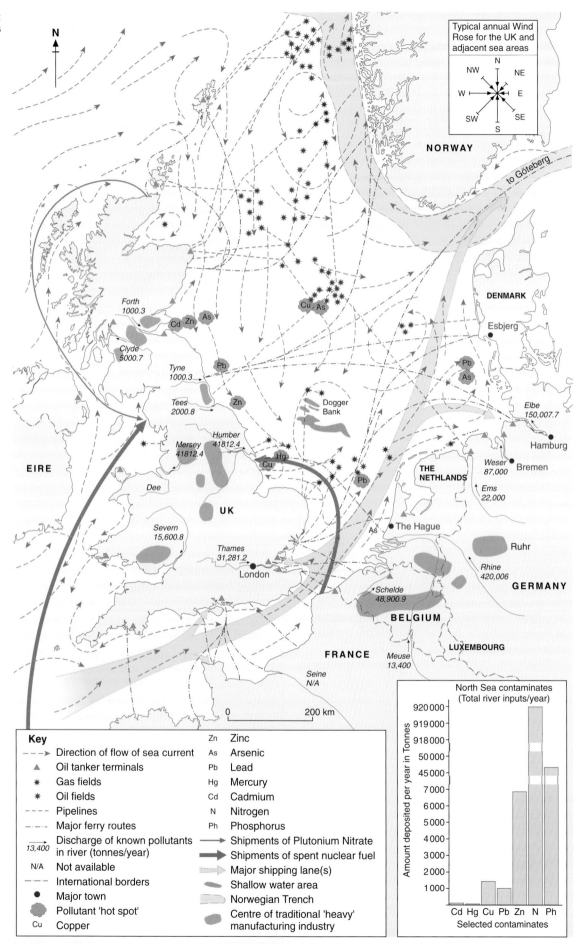

Key

- - - → Direction of flow of sea current
▲ Oil tanker terminals
✳ Gas fields
✳ Oil fields
- - - Pipelines
-·-·- Major ferry routes
↗ Discharge of known pollutants
13,400   in river (tonnes/year)
N/A Not available
-·-·- International borders
● Major town
⬢ Pollutant 'hot spot'
Cu Copper

Zn Zinc
As Arsenic
Pb Lead
Hg Mercury
Cd Cadmium
N Nitrogen
Ph Phosphorus

→ Shipments of Plutonium Nitrate
➡ Shipments of spent nuclear fuel
⬜ Major shipping lane(s)
⬬ Shallow water area
⬜ Norwegian Trench
⬤ Centre of traditional 'heavy'
   manufacturing industry

Typical annual Wind
Rose for the UK and
adjacent sea areas

North Sea contaminates
(Total river inputs/year)

FIGURE 4.6.4 Source: SUNDAY TIMES, 4 March 1990

North Sea chokes to death on its filth

Rivers, so damaged by chemicals that they are biologically dead in places, are pouring millions of tonnes of sewage and industrial pollutants into the North Sea. The Scheldt, Europe's dirtiest river, supplies the sea with raw sewage from the 1.6 m inhabitants of Brussels.

This sewage, and the industrial effluent of at least 1500 Belgian companies illegally discharging chemicals, pours untreated into the river Senne and, via the Scheldt, into the North Sea near the holiday beaches of Knokke.

Many scientists believe that pollution is spreading up the food chain from microscopic organisms to sea mammals such as seals and, eventually, humans. In some areas, including those used by Britain as sites for dumping and burning industrial waste, more than half the fish are showing acute signs of disease and malformation. In other parts algal blooms, caused by nitrates and phosphates from sewage and intensive farming, having sucked oxygen out of the water and killed all marine life.

The dangers to human health have had their effects on Jeff Smith, a fish merchant in Seaham, County Durham, who now travels 100 miles north to Scotland each week to buy shellfish because of contamination in his local supplies. Colliery waste has blackened his local coastline. 'The crabs are in such a dirty condition they are inedible,' he said. 'When any attempt is made to remove the stomach a black, tarry-looking liquid is emitted.'

Warnings about the deteriorating state of the North Sea have gone largely unheeded since 1967, when an international team of scientists advised drastic action after witnessing the biological deaths of parts of the Great Lakes in North America and Lake Geneva in Switzerland. The main obstacle to political initiative has been that the sea is the common property of the eight nations whose shorelines it touches and, as such, is regarded as nobody's individual responsibility.

Britain, the country most commonly labelled the dirty man of Europe, has tried to delay action every time North Sea countries have met to discuss the problems since 1972. Even when other countries began enforcing strict pollution controls in the mid-1980s, Britain still insisted that the sea 'flushed' itself clean.

Low-waste manufacturing methods, recycling, the use of non-toxic substitutes and more sophisticated treatment – many already in use in the United States – could end much of the problem.

Three years ago when the eight North Sea countries – Britain, France, Belgium, Holland, West Germany, Denmark, Sweden and Norway – met in London, they proposed to reduce North Sea pollution by 50% by 1995. But, according to an independent report by international lawyers to be published by Greenpeace this week, none of those eight is likely to achieve all of their promises by then.

Source: *Sunday Times*, 4 March 1990

Greenpeace North Sea campaign in the 1980s

Prior to its first North Sea campaign in 1980, Greenpeace had no clear idea which pollution issues it needed to target most urgently.

In the spring of 1980, Greenpeace learned from its Dutch office that liquid containing lead, cadmium and mercury was being regularly shipped down the Rhine from dye factories at Leverkusen which were owned by the German chemical company Bayer; the liquid was then discharged at sea from two specially-equipped dump ships. Greenpeace's response was to immobilize these two ships by chaining inflatable dinghies to their rudders and waste discharge pipes!

Greenpeace supporters in Germany then blockaded ships engaged in the transportation of titanium dioxide waste from factories belonging to the American-owned company Kronos-Titan. This chemical had been used as a whitener in paint since the 1960s, but the process used to extract the titanium oxide from its ore was very inefficient and its waste contained acids and heavy metals; when dumped, the waste turned the sea white. Greenpeace adopted the campaign in December 1980, demanded that titanium dioxide dumping should cease by the end of 1985, and started to

collect detailed evidence of its effects on marine life. In 1982, the Netherlands announced that Kronos-Titan would have to halve its dumping of titanium dioxide waste. Greenpeace's campaign was clearly beginning to achieve positive results – after only two years of sustained action!

By 1983, Greenpeace's campaign issues had been

STUDENT ACTIVITY 4.10

1 Describe how the three graphs in Figure 4.6.1 highlight the complexity of North Sea pollution inputs.

2 With the help of Figures 4.6.2–4:

(a) outline the various ways in which the North Sea is being polluted, adding the names of those countries and rivers most concerned in each case; this information could be laid out as a table or in the form of an essay.

(b) suggest some of the adverse economic effects of the pollution types which you have just outlined.

(c) explain how natural atmospheric and hydrospheric systems combine to make pollution in the North Sea a truly international problem.

widened to include ocean incineration, the effects of PCBs, the French dumping of gysum sludge and the continuing British dumping of sewage.

By 1986, Greenpeace was becoming very concerned about the role which the UK would play at the forthcoming Second North Sea Conference in London. In fact, there was growing suspicion that the UK had offered to host the conference merely so that it could 'dilute' the conference's objectives; whilst much of Europe already recognised that the only realistic approach was to attack pollution problems at source, the UK still insisted that corrective measures should be taken only when the sea's pollution tolerance limits had already been exceeded. Greenpeace promptly decided to expose the UK as the 'dirty man of Europe' and create enough political pressure to force the government to review its policy.

Meanwhile, Greenpeace was intensifying its own research activities – using the new laboratory ship *BELUGA*. At about the same time, European politicians were busy assessing the findings of their own 'Quality Status Report'. These findings convinced the politicians that the North Sea was *already* heavily polluted. The report argued that scientists could never determine exactly how much any sea could absorb and the Second North Sea Conference responded by adopting what is now widely known as the 'precautionary principle'.

It was clear that neither the French nor the Belgians would support the UK at the conference and the official welcoming speech made by the Prince of Wales on 14 November 1987 had a profound effect on the UK delegates; he chose to present his own view very effectively in the form of a metaphor: 'While we wait for the doctor's diagnosis, the patient may easily die'. His strident words of warning were widely reported in the British press and, *the very next day*, the UK government formally supported the precautionary principle as the wisest approach to the problem of North Sea pollution! The UK also agreed to reduce – before the end of 1995 – all discharges of nutrients and particularly dangerous substances by 50 per cent of their 1985 levels.

The Greenpeace campaign against the incineration of hazardous waste at sea also gained momentum at about that time. The campaign had been launched in 1982 – following the discovery that the incineration vessel *MATTHIAS II* was emitting deadly dioxins. Its activities had earlier provoked Greenpeace to demand that the ship be withdrawn from the North Sea area, partly on the grounds that incinerator emissions harmed fish larvae feeding near the surface. This led to the decision at the Second North Sea Conference to stop all maritime waste incineration by the end of 1984. By early 1989, pressure on the North Sea states to agree an earlier date had reached an extraordinary pitch and, shortly afterwards, Belgium became the first of the states to ban the practice.

Greenpeace recognised that political arguments at the Third North Sea Conference would be won or lost as much on scientific grounds as through environmental campaigning. It therefore commissioned experts to discover how successful each country had been in meeting the pollution reduction commitments which it had made at the Second Conference. They reported that, in most cases, these objectives were far from being met. Early in 1989, the Dutch government fell – over the issue of how the protection of the environment should be funded. The Swedish government was also forced into premature elections in spring 1989, and lost.

In 1988, Greenpeace adopted the slogan 'Zero 2000' in support of its campaign to stop *all* pollution entering the North Sea by the end of the century. In its five-minute address allowed by conference rules, Greenpeace argued for further reductions in pollution – reductions which would ultimately lead to the eradication of all significant water contamination by 2000. Three weeks after the conference, the European Parliament passed a resolution calling for zero discharges into the North Sea by the end of the millenium.

As the North Sea provides one of the classic examples of international pollution, it seems inevitable that environmental improvements within this area will only be achieved by means of whole-region co-operation. It is also important to acknowledge the role played by environmental pressure groups and local communities affected by pollution problems. The contribution of Greenpeace is especially noteworthy and an account of its initiatives in North West Europe is therefore also included (see page xx).

Technology is being used increasingly to identify and quantify pollution incidents and a three-year satellite monitoring programme begun in December 1996 has been effective in monitoring pollution levels and identifying newly polluted areas. It was then able to direct specially-equipped 'response' aircraft and ships to problem areas where they could collect evidence sufficiently detailed to be used as evidence in court proceedings against the organisations responsible for the outbreaks of pollution which it had identified. It could also track 'natural' phenomena such as algal blooms and illegal spillages of oil, chemicals and effluent. This 'Clean Seas Project' was a truly international effort, as it co-ordinated the work and expertise of many European research units (e.g. Hamburg University and Southampton Oceanography Centre).

International Conferences on the Protection of the North Sea

(the 'North Sea Conferences')

The First Conference, at Bremen, in 1984:
1 Stressed the importance of existing international bodies and treaties, e.g. The Oslo Convention on Dumping at Sea, the Paris Convention on Pollution from Land-based Sources and the International Maritime Organisation (IMO) on shipping issues.

2 Approved the structure of future conferences, by which government ministers would give guarantees of future action and provide feed-back on the progress made to fulfil previously agreed strategies.

The Second Conference, at London, in 1987:
1 Agreed to adopt the 'precautionary principle', by which the environment must always be assumed to be at risk – even when the scientific evidence needed to prove this is not available.
2 Agreed discharge reductions of especially toxic substances and nutrients to 50 per cent of their 1985 levels by 1995; also to end dumping of all industrial waste at sea by 1989; and to stop all offshore incineration of waste by 1994.
3 Agreed to establish a Scientific Task Force to co-ordinate research into North Sea pollution issues.

The Third Conference, at The Hague, in 1990:
1 Agreed the principle that discharges of toxic substances capable of entering the marine environment should be reduced before the year 2000 to levels which are not considered harmful to man or nature.
2 Agreed 50–70 per cent reductions in discharges of 36 Priority Hazardous Substances such as dioxins; 170 less toxic substances were placed on a 'Reference List' for later discussion.
3 Identified 34 pesticides as needing to be phased out of use; also discussed pesticide control measures.
4 Discussed a wide range of other environmental problems and measures, e.g. with respect to the dumping and incineration of waste at sea, radio-active waste and the phasing-out of PCBs.
5 The UK agreed to stop sewage sludge dumping by 1998.

The Fourth Conference, at Esbjerg, in 1995:
1 Accepted that North Sea fishery issues should form part of conference business.
2 Discussed issues concerning individual marine species and their habitats.
3 Tightened controls on the run-off of nutrients from intensive farming areas; discharge levels of radioactive substances were also discussed.
4 The threat of pollution from ships and offshore installations was highlighted as a cause of major concern.

STUDENT ACTIVITY 4.11

1 Outline the main outcomes of each of the four North Sea Conferences.
2 Read the Greenpeace campaign summary carefully, then note down its main points under the following three headings:
■ campaign themes
■ strategies used to achieve stated aims
■ successful outcomes.
3 In most major respects, the Mediterranean Sea is just as much at risk from pollution inputs as the North Sea. Your objective is to create a fact-file having the title 'Pollution Issues in the Mediterranean Sea'. The file could be sub-divided into three sections, each outlined below:
Section 1 – The Mediterranean Basin.
Consult atlas maps to produce a summary of its physical characteristics (e.g. size and depth) and reasons why it takes at least 80 years for rivers and adjacent sea areas to 'flush' out pollutants completely.
Section 2 – Pollution Risks.
Use atlases and reference texts to obtain a profile of the human characteristics of the Mediterranean Region (e.g. population concentrations and growth trends, industrial regions, tourist honeypots and shipping routes) and use this collected information to predict how and where this sea is most at risk from pollution. It may be helpful to first discuss and then 'pool' your individual findings.
Section 3 – Pollution Control Strategies.
Use GDP figures to assess the relative ability of the Mediterranean states to finance control strategies. Finally, use the Internet to investigate 'The Blue Plan' agreement of 1979.

5

ATMOSPHERIC POLLUTION — *THE GLOBAL ISSUE*

5.1 *The nature of the atmosphere*

It has been common knowledge for some years that a phenomenon known as **global warming** has been influencing the earth's climatic systems. The monitoring of temperature changes indicates that the 'average global temperature' has risen by 0.5°C over the last 100 years; parallel observations have traced a number of significant changes in the relative composition of the major atmospheric gases

(Figure 5.1.1). Our knowledge of the crucial role played by each of these gases in stabilising global temperatures is sufficient for linkages between all these trends to be established with a high degree of confidence. The processes involved in these linkages have been termed **the greenhouse effect** and **ozone depletion** (Figure 5.1.2).

FIGURE 5.1.1 Global warming factors

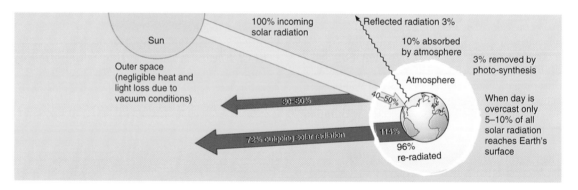

FIGURE 5.1.2 Ozone depletion factors

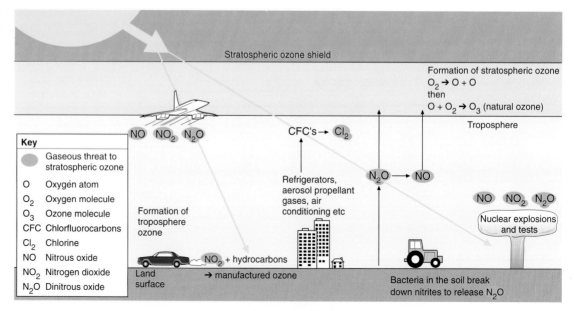

STUDENT ACTIVITY 5.1

1 All parts of this question are based on the two diagrams and the three standard terms on page 70.

(a) Draw a pie graph to show the composition of the earth's atmosphere.

(b) Explain why it is important that this particular composition should not change significantly; include the terms greenhouse effect, global warming and ozone depletion in your answer and use each term in such a way that you make clear your understanding of the processes and hazards involved.

(c) What measures are likely to prove effective in combating each of the hazards which you have just described?

(d) Assess the likelihood of success being achieved for each of the measures which you outlined in answer to (c) above. To answer this question with conviction, you should try to avoid vague generalisations – by quoting specific difficulties whenever possible.

2 Refer to Figure 5.1.3 to answer the following questions about alternative energy sources:

(a) Suggest reasons why wind power is currently the British Government's favoured option.

(b) What major disadvantages are shared by wind, wave and tidal power?

(c) List at least eight 'location factors' which should influence the siting of conventional (i.e. not pumped-storage) hydro-electric power stations. You will need to include a number of factors relating to the geology and relief of suitable locations.

FIGURE 5.1.3 Classic locations for selected 'alternative energies'

5.2 *Localised air pollution*

Whilst air pollution often involves entire regions, this unit examines an incident which occurred so far from any country boundaries that its effects were restricted not only to a single country, but also a particular part of it – the state of Madhya Pradesh, in central India.

What is often referred to as 'the world's worst industrial accident' occurred on 2 December, 1984, in the Indian city of Bhopal. The factory involved was a Union Carbide pesticide-manufacturing plant, around which a large area of densely-populated, poor-quality housing had previously developed. The following casualty and consequence statistics indicate why the tragedy is often referred to in such highly emotive language.

■ The official death toll now stands at almost 10 000. Figures provided by the Welfare Commissioner's office in Bhopal listed 5325 fatalities up to the end of 1992, but this figure may well be an under-estimate and all are agreed that the number of casualties continues to rise. The

official death toll within the first two weeks of the accident was 2500, but more victims have died since than during the first phase of the disaster. The quoted figures are, however, very unreliable – because they fail to take into account a substantial number of corpses which were removed from the scene by government trucks without having first being counted! Also unrecorded were some inevitable deaths among the 400 000 people who migrated from Bhopal to escape gas poisoning. 16 000 appears to be a much more reliable estimate of the total of exposure-related deaths;

■ According to the Indian Council of Medical Research, 521 000 people suffered exposure to the toxic gas and have since been proved to be affected physically in some way. However, there has been a long-term official ban on the publication of ICMR reports, which leads one to believe that this figure should also be considered an under-estimate;

■ The toxins from the factory entered victims' blood streams through the lungs and then

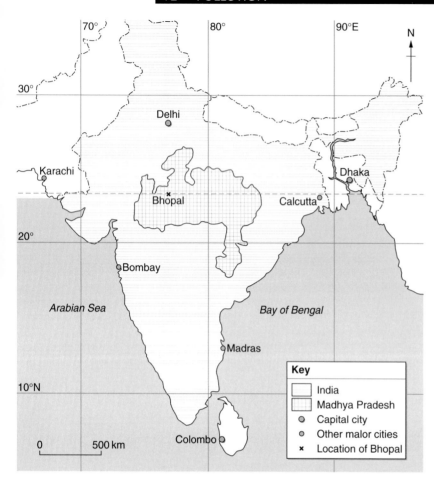

FIGURE 5.2.1 Location of Bhopal, India

leakage took place from an underground storage tank. When water accidentally entered this tank, its cooling system failed, causing the reaction mixture first to overheat and then explode. Once in the atmosphere, some of the MIC gas was converted to even more deadly hydrogen cyanide. The cloud of toxic gases settled over some 78 square kilometres and exposed up to 600 000 people – many of whom were destitute squatters who had settled there simply because they had nowhere else to go.

A heated debate to apportion blame for the Bhopal Disaster continues to the present time. Indian government officials claim that the accident was caused by negligence on the part of the company. Union Carbide representatives maintain that sabotage was the primary cause. The economic damage caused has been estimated at over $2.5 billion. Other estimates indicate that an additional investment in plant safety of only £0.6 million might well have prevented the disaster. The Indian Government initially demanded that Union Carbide should pay compensation amounting to £1.5 billion, but a much lower figure of £470 million was subsequently approved by the Indian Supreme Court. The government did not begin to pay compensation to individuals until eight years after the disaster and many victims still only receive compensation at a rate of £5 per month. Most of the poor people who lived closest to the plant were not able to keep written records of their ailments – records which could have provided vital support for their medical claims for compensation. There is evidence that some of the wealthier residents bribed their doctors to provide exaggerated accounts of their suffering – to enable them to claim greater but totally unjustified compensation. Survivors' organisations have since called for the creation of a National Medical Commission on Bhopal to oversee medical care and research as well as the monitoring of the health of survivors, but the Indian government appears unwilling to consider this suggestion.

progressed to various parts of the body. Once well-established there, they damaged vital organs (see Figure 5.2.4) and rendered the victims more vulnerable to secondary infection. Children appear to have been at particular risk and become two to four times more likely to experience fever, breathlessness, vomiting and coughing. It also seems likely that the next generation of babies will suffer some serious genetic defects. Academic research based on neighbouring communities indicates that 65 per cent of the population under review continue to have difficulty breathing, 50 per cent have eye problems and over 40 per cent experience reproductive disorders. Even now, 4000 victims on average seek medical help every day at Bhopal's government-run hospitals;

■ Lack of body energy means that large numbers of victims can no longer undertake physically-demanding work; this seriously weakens their ability to support their families. Workers in Bhopal's textile and paper mills have since been particularly prone to absence from work. The survivors have been forced to buy medicines which they can ill-afford, thus leaving even less money for food and clothing. Loss of income has also forced people to resort to local money-lenders, whose annual rates of interest may exceed *200* per cent!

The original cause of the disaster was a leakage of 40 tonnes of highly toxic methyl isocyanate (MIC) gas – a vital ingredient in the manufacture of carbamate agricultural pesticides. The initial

---

STUDENT ACTIVITY 5.2

1 Describe the situation of Bhopal relative to both its state and country boundaries.
2 (a) Investigate, then debate and describe, the climatic (especially wind) patterns which operate within central India.
(b) What is the relevance, if any, of the timing of the Bhopal Disaster with respect to the climatic patterns you have just described?
3 What lessons may be learned from the Bhopal Disaster? You are advised to itemise your answer under a series of appropriate sub-headings such as:

■ company investment and safety precautions
■ medical implications
■ national government responsibilities
■ individual family responsibilities.

Damage to eyes including:- partial/complete blindness, chronic conjunctivitis, early cataracts and poor vision

Damage to lungs e.g. emphysema and chronic bronchitis leading to breathlessness and coughing. Also, transfer of toxins (which were inhaled) into the blood

Menstural problems

Other side effects:
1 Neurological disorders including memory disfunction and reduced motor skills
2 Musculo-skeletal problems
3 General debility and lethargy
4 Impaired immune system

Psychological problems including:- distress, anxiety and depression. Post-traumatic stress disorders.

High temperature

Gastro-intestinal problems including:- vomitting, hyperacidity and chronic gastritis

Possible weight loss due to lack of food (because of other side-effects)

Reproductive disfunction including an increase in spontaneous abortions and still births. Genetic impairment in children.

FIGURE 5.2.4 Medical problems caused by the explosion at Bhopal

FIGURE 5.2.3 Densely-populated squatter settlements adjacent to the Bhopal plant

FIGURE 5.2.2 Bhopal Pesticide Manufacturing Plant

FIGURE 5.2.5 Victim of the Bhopal disaster

5.3 Acid rain

So-called 'acid rain' is a phenomenon caused primarily by the burning of fossil fuels. Electricity generating power stations are the chief source of sulphur dioxide (SO_2), while vehicle exhaust emissions contain the other most important source gases – nitrogen oxides (NOx). As the number of each type of source increased, so did the combined volume of their pollutant gases. Their potential for pollution is further increased by atmospheric inter-reactions between these primary pollutants, aided by the presence of direct sunlight. The resultant cocktail of pollutant gases then dissolves in precipitation-forming moisture, which returns to ground level in the form of acidic rain, snow, sleet or hail. These often indicate acidity levels far in excess of 7.0 pH – the norm for 'clean' rain or vapour which has just evaporated from a water surface. Acidity levels due to pollution in the 4.6–5.6 pH range are most common, while the highest ever recorded was 2.4 pH – at Pitlochrie, in Scotland. As rain is the dominant form of precipitation, 'acid rain' proved to be the inevitable choice of term for this phenomenon.

The existence of acid rain was first identified in 1872, as a result of observations on air pollution in Manchester carried out by the Scottish scientist Robert Angus Smith. The first consequences of its precipitation were, however, observed much later – in Scandinavia in the early 1970s. Its effects became progressively more damaging and widespread as the emissions of sulphur and nitrogen increased. Its most serious consequences (which relate to natural vegetation, the marine environment and structures such as buildings and statues) are illustrated in Figure 5.3.1.

FIGURE 5.3.1 Forest degradation caused by acid rain

FIGURE 5.3.2 A helicopter dumps lime into a lake in Sweden to neutralise the acid that is killing it

Acid rain is essentially a regional problem, which makes an effective human response easier to achieve than in the case of those pollution issues of a truly global-scale examined in the next unit. European co-operation to combat acid rain has proved to be one of the more encouraging anti-pollution campaigns of recent decades – despite the often heated debates which have occurred between individual states.

In the late 1970s, the United Nations Economic Commission for Europe (UNECE) established an international convention for the purpose of investigating long-range, trans-boundary air pollution. By the mid 1980s, most UNECE member

FIGURE 5.3.3 Statue degraded by acid rain

Key
A Albania
Ar Armenia
Az Azerbaijan
Be Belgium
De Denmark
Es Estonia
Sw Switzerland
L Luxembourg
Lich Lichtenstein
Lith Lithuania
M Moldova
Ma Macedonia
Mo Montenegro
Ne Netherlands
S Slovenia

Key Tonnes of sulphur and nitrogen deposits per hectare

- above 3.0
- 2.6 – 3.0
- 2.1 – 2.5
- 1.6 – 2.0
- 1.1 – 1.5
- 0.6 – 1.0
- 0.0 – 0.5

FIGURE 5.3.4 Acid rain levels: Western Europe (1990)

countries had agreed to reduce their sulphur dioxide emissions by 30 per cent of their 1980 levels – which led to them being nick-named 'The 30 per cent Club'. All these countries have since met their agreed reduction targets – the UK attaining a 35 per cent reduction, while Austria achieved an impressive 82 per cent. In 1994, a second phase of sulphur dioxide reductions was agreed – its cumulative targets being a 70–80 per cent reduction of 1980 levels by the turn of the century for the Western European countries and 49–50 per cent for those in Eastern Europe.

Planned reductions have been made possible by less reliance on fossil fuels for electricity generation and fitting emission filtration equipment to selected power stations. More localised initiatives have included lime-spraying to neutralise the acidity of the most affected lakes, particularly in southern Scandinavia (see Figure 5.3.4). A British example of successful lime application is Loch Fleet, in South West Scotland. Loch Fleet was teeming with trout before becoming biologically dead during the early 1980s. Intensive applications of lime to the loch and its surrounding moorland and forests over a five year period (costing £1.5 million and funded jointly by the three British electricity boards, British Coal and the Swedish State Power Board) have accelerated the recovery of the lake – which would have taken more than a century to achieve without human intervention. A further measure, which appears to be gaining increasing popularity, is the imposition of a 'carbon tax' on polluters; such a scheme would almost certainly operate on a sliding scale, so that the more serious offenders would pay significantly higher rates of taxation.

FIGURE 5.3.5 Acid rain-related factors in selected Western Europe countries

Country	Annual Sulphur deposition (×1000 tonnes)	Annual Nitrogen Dioxide emissions (×1000 tonnes)	Carbon Dioxide emissions (tonnes per capita)	Precipitation pH	Energy production (millions of tonnes of oil equivalent)	% of energy produced from solid fuels and petroleum products	Average no. of passenger cars per 100 people
Belgium	152	62	10.4	5.3	11.6	28.4	39
Denmark	78	45	9.9	4.5	8.9	96.6	31
France	568	362	6.3	4.7	97.3	10.8	42
Germany	1948	803	10.5	4.6	182.7	60.4	48
Ireland	78	32	8.8	5.2	3.3	71.7	23
Netherlands	84	71	9.0	4.8	59.7	45.8	37
Norway	18	94	9.0	4.4	120.2	1.0	38
Poland	1362	822	9.6	4.3	97.3	98.3	14
Sweden	50	161	5.8	4.6	29.6	5.9	42
UK	1597	430	9.8	4.8	203.1	73.4	37

STUDENT ACTIVITY 5.3

1 Make an enlarged copy of the diagram at the bottom of this page, then complete it by adding further arrow-labels to indicate the pH levels for:
- 'clean' rain
- the average acidity of precipitation on the two European countries most affected by acid rain in 1990
- the average acidity of precipitation on the two European countries least affected by acid rain, also in 1990
- the highest precipitation acidity ever recorded.

2 Using a method of your own choice, display a wide range of information related to the *sources*, *processes* and *outcomes* involved in the creation of acid rain in Western Europe. This could be achieved with a simple diagram comprising three columns headed by the three words highlighted above *in italics*. An alternative (and somewhat more challenging!) method is to design a flow diagram with direction arrows linking its information boxes. Students having artistic talents could create a fully-labelled, oblique-aerial 'landscape' diagram which incorporates sketches of power stations, vehicular transport, atmospheric processes, forests, lakes and other components in the acid rain sequence. Figure 3.3.3 on page 32 provides information about some of the chemical processes involved in the early stages in the formation of acid rain.

3 (a) Describe the pattern of acid rain distribution shown in Figure 5.3.6.
(b) Comment on the closeness of any links between your description for 3(a) and the tabled information given in Figure 5.3.7. You should quote precise figures wherever appropriate to support your observations.
(c) Account for any significant similarities and

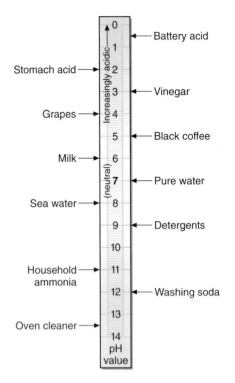

FIGURE 5.3.6 For use with Question 1

differences which you included in your comments for 3(b).
4 Outline the main ways by which the problems associated with acid rain might be reduced, then use the data given in this unit to assess the overall effectiveness of such measures.
5 The north-eastern states of the USA represent another region where acid rain-related problems are especially severe. Using information which you yourself have obtained, summarise the chief reasons for such problems in this particular region.

5.4 *The global dimension*

The Rio Earth Summit took place in the Brazilian city of Rio de Janeiro in June, 1992. Its two chief purposes were to assess the current state of the natural environment and monitor progress on development issues since the 1972 United Nations Conference on the Human Environment in Stockholm.

The Rio Conference was officially named The United Nations Conference on Environment and Development (UNCED), but became more popularly known as 'The Earth Summit' – in recognition of the global scale of its agenda and the fact that no fewer than 178 countries participated, 120 of them represented by their heads of state. The

summit was also remarkable for the fact that over 1000 non-governmental organisations (NGOs) took part – one-third of them from developing countries – and the first occasion on which 'unofficial' groups such as Greenpeace were in a position to exert influence on a world scale. Furthermore, it was the first major environmental conference to take place without the stresses of superpower conflict which had dominated world politics during the 'Cold War' stalemate of the 1950s–80s.

A dominant theme of the summit was **sustainable development**, defined in the Brundtland Report of 1987 as 'development which meets the needs of the present without compromising the ability of future generations to meet their own needs'. Sustainable development therefore featured in many of the recommended outcomes of this summit. Its most noteworthy achievements were two Conventions – on Climate Change and on **Biological Diversity** – both internationally-binding agreements which countries were expected to act upon without first having to draft their own internal legislation.

The primary aim of the Climate Convention was to stabilise the concentrations of greenhouses gases within the atmosphere – a major factor in fluctuations within the global climate pattern. This convention highlighted low-lying coastal or island areas, areas prone to desertification and fragile mountain ecosystems as being at particular risk, then summed-up the more general situation very clearly: 'The global nature of climate change requires the widest possible co-operation by all countries and their participation in an effective and appropriate international response'. Unfortunately, subsequent progress in this key area has fallen well short of that anticipated by the conference, as the following selected statistics show all too clearly:

■ In 1996, global carbon emissions reached a record annual level of 6.25 billion tonnes, which is at least 2 billion tonnes more than the world's forests and oceans can absorb annually. The United States alone contributes 23 per cent of the total global production of carbon – even though its population represents a mere 5 per cent of all humanity;

■ CO_2 emissions from the United States have increased by 8 per cent since the Earth Summit; they are expected to be 13 per cent above the 1990 level by the turn of the century. The equivalent figures for Japan and the EU will exceed 6 per cent;

■ Emissions of CO_2 by the **rapidly industrialising nations** such as China, Brazil and Indonesia will exceed their 1990 levels by 20–40 per cent;

■ The 1990s seem certain to be the hottest decade on record. In 1995, a United Nations panel of 2500 scientists agreed that human activity is already significantly affecting global climatic systems.

The Biodiversity Convention aimed to conserve the present range of biological resources, partly in order to sustain our ability to utilise its valuable components; it insisted that the benefits and profits which result from resource application (e.g. increased food yields and the development of more effective medicines) should be shared equitably between all countries involved; it also required individual countries to make an inventory of their biological resources and to increase protection for key natural areas. One hundred and sixty eight countries have since ratified this treaty, but the United States has, as yet, failed to do so. Two statistics indicating a global failure to implement the Biodiversity Convention principles effectively are:

'Listen to this, Lizzie. A piece of ice bigger than Norfolk has broken away from Antarctica'

FIGURE 5.4.1 Global warming appears certain to have wide-ranging impacts on most of the world's population!

■ It is estimated that more than 100 000 plant and animal species were lost in the five years since the Earth Summit took place;

■ The loss of forest habitats continues at the alarming rate of 13.7 million hectares per year (equivalent to half the combined land area of England, Scotland and Wales).

The most notable failure of the Rio Summit also concerned forest issues. It had been hoped that a third 'convention-type' treaty might be achieved on this theme but the conference could only reach agreement on a '*Statement* of Forest Principles', whose 15 components were not legally-binding on the countries which signed it. These principles included measures to conserve forested areas and to promote sustainable patterns in the production and consumption of forest products. There was however one important stumbling block to achieving full treaty status – a common belief amongst the developing countries that treaty restrictions would seriously undermine their export trade of **primary products**, such as coffee and timber.

The 'Rio Declaration' (see page 78) incorporates the very wide range of topics discussed at the Earth Summit; it also indicates the generally positive approach adopted by delegates towards future international co-operation in developmental and environmental matters. These principles represent a genuine attempt by the conference as a whole to both direct and encourage people to work effectively towards a situation in which sustainable developments become the norm rather than the exception. It was the intention that individuals should work more closely together to achieve this situation – irrespective of their socio-economic status – at local, regional, national and international levels. The recommended means of implementing the 27 general principles appeared in a separate document called 'Agenda 21', which listed some 2000 more-detailed guidelines. Collectively, these guidelines provided governments with a

The Rio Declaration

1 The well-being of human populations is the chief concern of sustainable development programmes. All people are entitled to a healthy and productive life, *in harmony with nature*.

2 States have every right to exploit their own resources and in accordance with their own domestic resource policies; but states also have a duty to make sure that resource exploitation does not damage the environments of other states or areas.

3 Existing as well as new developments must not disregard the needs of both present and future generations.

4 In order to achieve sustainable development, environmental protection shall always be a part of *the development process*.

5 All states and peoples shall co-operate in the essential task of eliminating poverty – a fundamental requirement for effective sustainable development.

6 Priority shall be given to the particular needs of developing countries – especially those countries which are the least developed and the most environmentally vulnerable. International actions in the field of environment and development should, however, also address the interests and needs of all countries as a matter of course.

7 States shall co-operate to conserve, protect and restore the earth's ecosystem. The developed countries must acknowledge the special responsibility which they bear in the pursuit of sustainable development, due to the pressures which their societies place on the global environment.

8 In order to achieve sustainable development and a higher quality of life for all peoples, states should reduce and then eliminate their unsustainable patterns of production and consumption. They should also promote *appropriate demographic policies*.

9 States should support sustainable development by their willingness to exchange scientific and technical knowledge.

10 Environmental issues are best managed with the participation of all concerned individuals and groups of people. Citizens should have access to environmental information held by their public authorities – including information on hazardous materials and activities in their communities. Citizens should be given the opportunity to participate in decision-making processes. Access to judicial and administrative proceedings (including *redress and remedy*) shall be provided.

11 States shall introduce environmental legislation which is appropriate to local circumstances and has particular regard for the economic and social costs involved.

12 *Unilateral actions* to deal with environmental challenges should be avoided. Environmental measures addressing international or global problems should, as far as possible, be based on international agreement.

13 States shall introduce laws regarding liability and compensation for the victims of pollution and other environmental damage. States shall co-operate more fully to develop international laws regarding liability and compensation for the adverse effects of environmental damage.

14 States should discourage or prevent the transfer of any activities and substances which cause severe environmental degradation or are found to be harmful to human health.

15 The *precautionary approach* to environmental protection shall be applied by states, according to their capabilities. Where there are threats of serious or *irreversible damage*, lack of *full scientific certainty* shall not be used as a reason for postponing cost-effective measures to prevent environmental degradation.

16 National authorities should recognise the principle that the polluter should be expected to bear pollution costs.

17 An *environmental impact assessment* shall be undertaken for proposed activities which are likely to have a significant adverse impact on the environment.

18 States shall immediately notify other countries of any natural disasters or other emergencies which are likely to have a harmful effect on their environments. The international community shall make every effort to help countries so affected.

19 States shall provide adequate notice of activities which may have significant adverse *trans-boundary* environmental effects.

20 Women have a vital role to play in environmental management and development. Their full participation is essential to the achievement of sustainable development.

21 The creativity, ideals and courage of the world's youth should also be mobilised to enhance sustainable development.

22 Indigenous peoples have a vital role to play in environmental management and development because of their knowledge and traditional practices. States should recognise this and encourage their participation in sustainable development programmes.

23 The environmental and natural resources of people under oppression, domination and occupation shall be protected.

24 Warfare is *inherently destructive* of sustainable development. States shall therefore respect international law by protecting the environment in times of armed conflict.

25 Peace, development and environmental protection are inseparable.

26 States shall resolve their environmental disputes peacefully and in accordance with the Charter of the United Nations.

27 States and people shall co-operate in good faith and in a spirit of partnership in the fulfilment of the principles embodied in this Declaration as well as in the further development of international law in the field of sustainable development.

blueprint for sustainable development which they could then incorporate within individual national policies.

Clearly, many of the key Earth Summit agreements have not been translated into effective action and the global ecosystem has continued to suffer as a direct result of this failure.

Is the chief cause of this overall failure due to a lack of determination on the part of the participating nations or, more worryingly, the result of strategies deliberately intended to frustrate the achievement of its goals? Many observers in the developing countries blame their wealthier counterparts for the failure of the global community to deliver; they accuse them of allowing short-term greed and self-interest to blind them to the much greater need to protect what all now accept is a most delicate environmental balance.

Agenda 21 has certainly heightened an awareness of the key issues involved on the part of both national governments and populations. It has also alerted individual communities to the dangerous consequences of *in*action. NGOs have been particularly active in applying pressure for change. All too often, however, their efforts have failed to force changes to national legislation which would make sustainable development an achievable goal early in the new millenium. It is in this context of global failure that the United Nations' Kyoto Summit on world climate was convened five years later.

The Kyoto Summit

Kyoto has been described as the most acrimonious and stressful environmental conference ever held! Its final (and most critical session) ended at 4 am on 11 December 1997 – with many of its weary delegates either sound asleep in chairs or slumped over their tables! Some were even lying on the floor, utterly exhausted by the debates and lobbying work of the previous week. What had created such prolonged tension that agreement could not be reached until the early hours of the very last morning? And was it worth all the effort?

Kyoto certainly kept the Rio Climate Convention alive – even if the rate of progress on the reduction of greenhouse gas emissions was far more modest than many countries would have wished (Figure 5.4.2). It is clearly well below the 60 per cent reduction in carbon dioxide which environmental groups believe is vital to stabilise the world's climates and allow its ecosystems to adapt fully to rising atmospheric temperatures. Indeed, a few countries were actually permitted to increase their emissions! Iceland, for example, had pleaded for special consideration because its relatively small emissions output would soon be increased anyway following the completion of a new aluminium smelter. Australia's case was based on the need to protect vital coal and steel industries. More significantly, none of the emissions targets agreed by the conference could become legally binding

until formally ratified by each of the 60 national governments involved! Al Gore, the US Vice-president, stated even before Kyoto's 10 000 delegates had left for home, that the Clinton administration would not consider putting the treaty to the Senate unless developing countries agreed to all its terms.

An 'emissions quota transfer system' was also agreed by the major industrialised nations, but the details of how this would operate and be monitored were not finalised in Kyoto. The extent of participation in the quota system by the Third World nations is as yet unclear, but it seems likely that these countries will succumb to the temptation to obtain desperately-needed extra income by bartering their own quotas on the international market!

The so-called 'carbon club' of petroleum companies such as BP, Esso and Shell – as well the major car manufacturers (e.g. Ford and General Motors) and the coal, steel and aluminium industries – were all delighted by Kyoto; the finally agreed targets for greenhouse gas emissions proved to be much more modest than they had dared hope for. They even felt sufficiently confident to predict that it would be 'business as usual' for their companies over the 12 year period covered by the Kyoto Treaty.

The American government was equally delighted that a system of 'emission quotas' would allow heavily-polluting countries to trade off their own emissions with others which achieved reduced emissions. Figure 5.4.3 illustrates how the quota system was expected to operate. The United States' enthusiasm for emissions-trading on a global scale was, in fact, based on previous experience in its own domestic power generation market. From the early 1990s, sulphur dioxide emission 'pollution permits' had been issued to individual American power stations – based on their current emissions status. Under this system, power stations which had invested in technology to cut emissions such as flue gas de-sulphurisation equipment, or buy more expensive coal having a lower sulphur content,

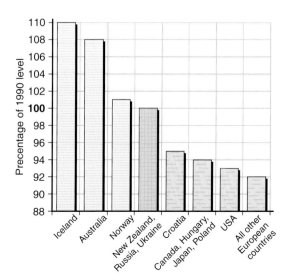

FIGURE 5.4.2 Emission quotas agreed at the 1997 Kyoto summit

could gain extra credits – based on how many tonnes of sulphur dioxide they no longer released into the atmosphere. These credits could then be bought by other, less pollution-efficient generating companies wishing to buy them in order to continue operating. If a power station closed down and was replaced by one which produced minimal sulphur emissions, large credits became available to

FIGURE 5.4.3 Operation of the Kyoto Summit emissions quota system

offset the cost of new construction. The scheme incorporated incentives to invest in more environmentally-friendly plants and, as only part of each tonne of sulphur saved could be sold as a credit, it should have proved possible to achieve an overall national reduction in pollutant emissions.

In fact, the United States has continued to pollute excessively. Its track record in emission reduction is so poor that Robin Pellew, of the World Wide Fund for Nature felt obliged to complain: 'The US may be an economic superpower, but morally they are in the dark ages. They are holding the whole world to ransom'. He has a point, because the quota system will allow it to buy other countries' carbon emissions in order to continue polluting at a heavy rate. The economic collapse of the former Soviet Union countries has greatly reduced their emissions of greenhouse gases and makes them prime targets for quota acquisition by the USA.

The 33 countries subject to the Kyoto Summit accept agreed emissions targets and estimates of their current pollutant emissions.

Individual governments decide how best to allocate their total annual permitted emissions to national, industrial, transportation and energy-generation sectors. Major allowances are expected to be given to selected highly-pollutant plants such as steelworks and oil refineries. Widely dispersed sources of air pollution such as individual road vehicles and homes are excluded.

Industrial plants which exceed their allocated emissions targets are fined.

Plants may 'buy' emissions capacity from other plants within the same country. Plants which reduce their own emissions may similarly opt to 'sell' unused capacity to others unable to do so.

The 'Joint Implementation' Agreement allows nations to trade emissions quotas; this may be achieved by exchanges of currency, but nations may not benefit in this way from emissions reductions which are due solely to decreases in pollutant activity caused by economic recessions rather than planned initiatives.

National emissions targets reviewed annually, with the aim of reducing global emissions on a year-by-year basis.

Processes outlined in above boxes repeated during each successive 12-month period.

5.5 *The nuclear debate*

The exploitation of nuclear energy has prompted one of the greatest ethical dilemmas of modern times. Few would deny its ability to generate very large amounts of electricity at the expense of relatively minute quantities of a limited natural resource – uranium; the same amount of power can only be generated by burning 20 000 times as much coal. Also, nuclear generators do not add to the global challenges posed by the greenhouse effect and its associated problems. A number of

industrially advanced countries such as France and Japan have favoured the widespread use of nuclear energy (Figure 5.5.1), the latter country understandably so in view of its lack of native fossil fuel resources and a desire to maximise its net balance of payments through a reduction of imported fuels. The United Kingdom was the first country to build a nuclear power station capable of generating viable quantities of electricity – in October 1956, at Calder Hall (in the now renamed

Sellafield complex) on the Cumbrian coast. It constructed a series of plants, first in remote and latterly within more densely-populated areas (Figure 5.5.4), but has recently committed itself to a greater use of domestic resources such as its offshore gasfields in the North and Irish Seas and the development of alternative energies – wind power being the most favoured option at present.

Nuclear energy does, however, pose major environmental challenges. These were most dramatically highlighted by the Three Mile Island incident of March 1979 in the USA and the Chernobyl Disaster, which is the subject of this unit's case study. On a lesser scale, embarrassingly frequent reports of leakages of radioactive dust and waste into both local and regional environments have added to public concern about the generation of power by nuclear fission. Scare-stories about nuclear-related shortcomings are all too common and, while relatively minor in most individual cases, they have collectively heightened concerns about the industry's ability to maintain acceptable safety standards.

A typical example was the discovery in February 1998 of high levels of radioactivity in seagulls which had nested on the chimneys and in the piping of the Sellafield nuclear waste reprocessing plant. Another, almost fairy-tale account from the former Soviet Union, concerned laid-up nuclear-powered submarines of the Russian Arctic Fleet which relied totally on shore-generated electricity to maintain their reactor safety systems. The financially-bankrupt Russian Fleet was constantly in debt to its onshore power supplier, which eventually threatened to disconnect the crucial power supply to the submarine reactors – a measure which, if carried out, would have initiated melt-down followed by a full-scale radiation disaster. Further damage to public perception has been caused by the secrecy with which governments and generating companies alike have attempted to restrict the knowledge of incidents such as those typified by the selection of newspaper cuttings on pages 83–84. The high, but as yet unquantified cost of decommissioning redundant nuclear power stations, is a further major concern. Similarly worrying are the escalating cost of radioactive waste disposal and long-term uncertainties about the current levels of technology involved in this process. Recent estimates put the cost of decommissioning each nuclear power station at just under £1 billion.

The Chernobyl Disaster

On 26 April 1986, a catastrophic explosion took place in Unit 4 of the Chernobyl Nuclear Power Plant in the former Soviet Union – now the Ukranian Republic (Figure 5.5.2). Its primary cause was a runaway chain-reaction and subsequent fire in the reactor core; this blew off the concrete protective roof of the reactor building and ejected radioactive debris and dust sufficiently high into

Country	Percentage of national electricity output generated by nuclear power stations	
	1982	1992
Argentina	8	19
Belgium	46	59
Brazil	–	1
Bulgaria	29	34
Canada	12	17
Czech Republic	8	29
Finland	42	33
France	48	73
Germany	18	28
Hungary	10	48
India	1	2
Japan	18	24
Mexico	–	4
Netherlands	6	5
Pakistan	1	1
Russia	6	13
South Africa	–	6
South Korea	17	48
Spain	8	36
Sweden	37	52
Switzerland	28	40
Taiwan	18	38
UK	18	21
USA	12	22

the atmosphere for global wind belts to transport them great distances.

The disaster sequence was initiated when an emergency cooling system was deliberately turned off to allow an *unauthorised* safety experiment to proceed. Almost the entire suite of core control rods was then removed and the automatic safety devices (specifically designed to shut down the reactor should water and steam levels fall below normal operating levels) were also shut off – to prevent these vital systems 'spoiling' the experiment! A standby water pump to cool the reactor was turned on, but reduced power output meant that its vital water supply failed to reach the reactor. The lack of a second protective encasement shell – fitted as standard on Western-style reactor plants – greatly reduced the plant's ability to contain the force of the explosion. Once the fires had been extinguished, the shattered reactor was hastily encased in a concrete tomb (Figure 5.5.3) – at enormous personal risk to the crews involved, who were restricted to only 40 seconds exposure on each working visit.

Fifteen nuclear reactors of the basic Chernobyl design still operate in parts of the former Soviet Union, in addition to at least another ten plants built to what must be considered inferior design specifications by current operating standards. As it is neither technologically nor financially feasible to correct the inherent design faults in any of these plants, they represent a dormant threat of immense proportions to world safety. The scale of the major consequences of the Chernobyl explosion was huge:

FIGURE 5.5.1 Nuclear power station trends within selected 'nuclear' countries

FIGURE 5.5.2 Location of Chernobyl Nuclear Power Station, Ukraine

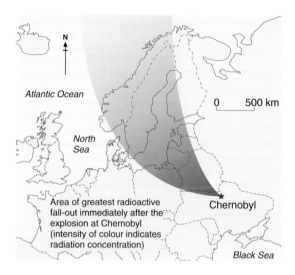

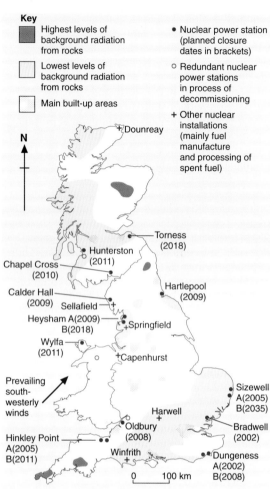

FIGURE 5.5.4 Location of Britain's nuclear power stations

FIGURE 5.5.3 Concrete 'tomb' sealing off the most seriously damaged part of Chernobyl Nuclear Power Station

■ The highly radioactive plume which entered the atmosphere comprised two chief components. Iodine-131 was mainly responsible for triggering cancer of the thyroid gland of local inhabitants, particularly children. Caesium-37, a much longer-living nuclide whose radioactivity decreases naturally by half only every 30 years, was the chief cause of whole-body radiation exposure over much of Europe and, to a lesser degree, throughout the northern hemisphere;

■ Many of the plant workers and the site restoration teams, known locally as 'liquidators', received particularly high doses of radiation. The official figures put the number of fatalities at only 45, but Greenpeace Ukraine maintain that the total death toll is likely to have exceeded 32 000;

■ Lethal radiation doses were observed in local ecosystems, most notably in voles – a stable diet of many predators higher up the food chain – as well as coniferous trees. Locally-produced foodstuffs were seriously contaminated in the short term, but certain wild-food products such as mushrooms, berries, game and fish from the most affected forests and lakes continue to pose a health hazard to humans. Wind-born radioactive fallout over large parts of Europe led to widespread precautionary measures, including the long-term isolation of entire flocks of sheep in upland regions of the British Isles such as Wales and the Lake District;

■ According to United Nations estimates, 375 000 Russians were forced to leave their homes, the majority never to return. Most of these people were not evacuated until 10 days after the explosion;

1 Describe the distribution of the United Kingdom's nuclear power generating plants as shown by Figure 5.5.2, then offer reasoned explanations in support of your description.
2 (a) Outline the chief causes and effects of the Chernobyl explosion.
(b) To what extent could both its causes and effects have been alleviated in the light of subsequent knowledge?
3 Debate the arguments both for and against the exploitation of nuclear energy – quoting detailed, factual information whenever appropriate. Conclude your debate with a summary of your *own* personal standpoint with regard to the ethics of nuclear power generation.

■ 160 000 square kilometres of the former Soviet Union remain contaminated with radioactivity;
■ The total cost to the Russian/Ukraine nations in terms of population resettlement, medical services, environmental protection measures and lost food and manufacturing production exceeds $250 billion. The long-term effects on the local national economies have been devastating. The President of Belarus, a neighbouring republic of Ukraine, has estimated the economic damage to his own country as 32 times the entire national annual budget; he also stated that 20–25 per cent of each annual State Budget still has to be allocated to post-Chernobyl corrective measures;
■ Delayed initial reactions to the explosion, and the degree of official secrecy which has surrounded it ever since, have unnecessarily heightened the consequences of the explosion and undermined the faith which the Soviet population had placed in nuclear generation.

Factors on nuclear leak withheld

Information about an accident at the Sellafield plant last week which showered nearby areas with radioactive dust was withheld for more than 36 hours. British Nuclear Fuels may face prosecution after failing to tell the Department of the Environment sooner.

The release, which was five times the company's average annual gaseous emissions and included plutonium dust, began on Wednesday and came from a 120 m chimney on the site. This is designed to dilute and disperse emissions, but because of the high pressure and air inversion it is believed that most of the plume was deposited in the Workington and Whitehaven areas.

Jack Cunningham, in the House of Commons yesterday, said there had been a totally unacceptable series of events.

The incident comes at an embarrassing time for Sellafield, which is facing prosecution for allegedly not taking proper safety precautions on its high-level waste processing plant. It is also trying to obtain new authorisations for discharges into the air. The release last Thursday and Friday exceeded the proposed new licence of discharges of 740 mega-becquerels and, if the licence had been issued, would have led to a prosecution.

Source: *Guardian*, 16 February 1993

Norway fury at UK

Norway has detected an eightfold increase in radioactive waste reaching its shores in the last year as a result of discharges from the Sellafield nuclear plant in Cumbria, and is to renew demands for the closure of the plant responsible.

The disclosure that the radionuclide Technetium-99 (T-99) has travelled 800 km on sea currents to the shores of Norway comes at an embarrassing time for the Government, which is considering an application for new discharge licences from the Sellafield plant.

Only three months ago Michael Meacher, the Environment Minister, at a meeting of ministers from 15 countries including Norway, pledged that the UK would end its sea discharges of nuclear waste and chemicals as soon as possible. It was to finally remove from Britain the tag of 'the dirty man of Europe'.

Thirteen of the countries present at the meeting of the Oslo/Paris Commission, which controls pollution in the North Sea, had expressed particular concern about T-99 because it accumulates in shellfish. Lobsters off Sellafield were caught in the summer by the Ministry of Agriculture (MAFF) and found to be 32 times above the European Union safe limit for human consumption.

Source: *Guardian*, 20 December 1997

FIGURE 5.5.5a Leaks at Sellafield

FIGURE 5.5.5b British nuclear waste reaches the shores of Norway

Nuclear timebomb on ro-ro ferry

Enough plutonium for up to 25 atomic bombs has been shipped around Britain in a roll-on roll-off ferry – and much more could follow.

The use of a ro-ro vessel, prone to capsize, is condemned by marine safety scientists and has outraged environmentalists.

The *Observer* has discovered that 83 kg of plutonium was sent from the Sellafield nuclear plant in Cumbria to a nuclear power station on the north coast of Germany in a ro-ro freight vessel, the *ARNFB*, in October last year.

The ship has been used three times since to transport 39 kg of plutonium from Hanau, in southern Germany, to the Dounreay nuclear plant on the north coast of Scotland.

BNFL, which operates Sellafield, is intending to process and return up to a further 12 tonnes of plutonium to Germany in the next 13 years. In June, the company was attacked by MPs for plans to fly the material. It now says that using a ro-ro ferry is an option.

The United Nations International Maritime Organisation says that ro-ro vessels are 'exceptionally vulnerable to human error' – they can sink quickly if their car decks are flooded with water. That is what happened to the *HERALD OF FREE ENTERPRISE* near Zeebrugge in 1987.

Carl Ross, professor of structural dynamics at Portsmouth University, believes that transporting plutonium in a ro-ro ferry is dangerous. 'It's most inadvisable,' he said. Recovering casks of plutonium from the seabed would be 'devishly difficult'.

Source: *Observer*, 23 November 1997

Dounreay exclusion zone for fishing

The Government banned fishing within two kilometres of Dounreay from eight o'clock last night, following the discovery of 34 fragments of irradiated nuclear fuel on the seabed this summer which were feared could enter the food chain.

Immediately, anti-nuclear campaigners issued urgent calls for an end to nuclear processing at the plant. They also want the Government to loosen the official gag on Dounreay's employees and former employees.

A Scottish Office statement said the ban was a precautionary measure based on advice from the Scottish Environment Protection Agency (Sepa). It would stay in force pending a full and detailed review by Sepa and the national Radiological Protection Board.

Sepa's north regions' director, Professor David MacKay, said yesterday the UK Atomic Energy Authority surveyed sandbanks off the plant during the Summer.

'They found a significant number of particles which were believed to be particles of radioactive rods that were processed in the 1960s. The numbers are sufficient that we believe that as a precautionary measure fishing should be banned until we can do a firm and solid assessment of what the risks actually are.'

Dounreay's director, Dr Roy Nelson, said last night: 'Over the past 40 years of operations Dounreay has carried out a systematic monitoring programme of the marine environment agreed with the relevant regulators who have assessed the results.

"No increase in radioactivity in seafood in recent years has been revealed by UKAEA monitoring or the independent monitoring carried out by Sepa or its predecessors. We have analysed 1000 lobsters and 30 000 crabs and never found a single particle in any of these.'

Source: *Herald*, 20 October 1997

6
LOCALITY STUDIES

Most of the units in Sections 2–5 of this book have concentrated on just one kind of pollution hazard. Many examination questions (see Unit 7.3 for examples) require candidates to demonstrate their breadth of knowledge by discussing *combinations* of hazards; these may be linked by type and/or location. A number of units which you have already studied, however, are based on more than one aspect of environmental pollution – particularly Unit 4.3, which investigates a useful range of pollutant sources including industry and agriculture, and Unit 4.6 on the 'cocktail effect' of a wide range of pollutants within the North Sea

6.1 *Lonsdale*

This unit provides a final opportunity to investigate multiple-hazard pollution – within a locality in North West England, known locally as Lonsdale, which includes the adjoining towns of Morecambe and Lancaster. This unit should also be viewed as an ideal opportunity to revise selected key pollution themes. Its chief information source is the 1:50 000 scale Ordnance Survey map extract of the study area on page 86; other visual resources are indicated in the instructions for Question 1.

The investigations which you are asked to do for Questions 2 and 3 are inevitably biased towards environmental difficulties which are likely to be experienced in the study locality. It does, therefore, require you to focus on potential problems rather than the many fine attributes which make the area so attractive to live in or visit. The brief summary which follows is included so that the reader may be able to view his/her perceived 'negative' issues within a balanced and realistic context.

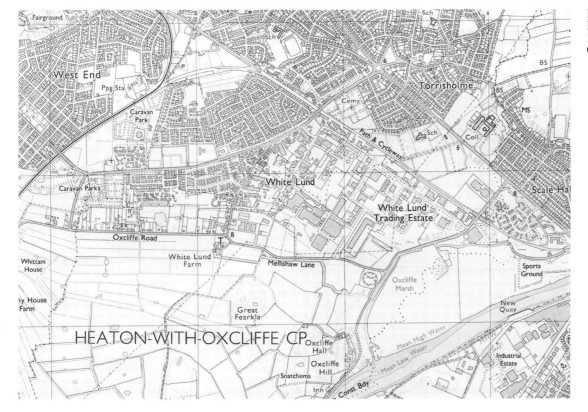

FIGURE 6.1.1 OS Map Extract 2: Pathfinder 1:25 000 sheet 648 © Crown copyright

FIGURE 6.1.2 OS Map
Extract 3: Landranger
1:50 000 sheet 97

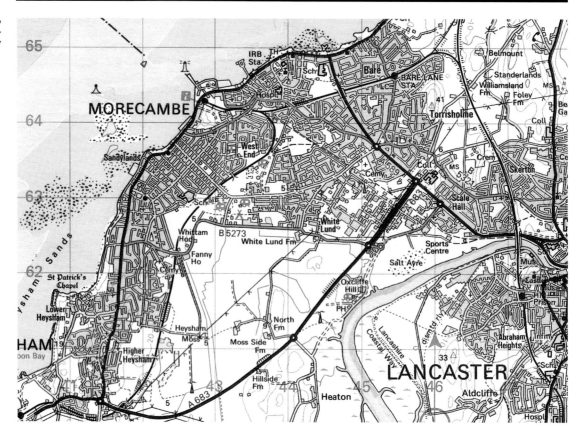

FIGURE 6.1.3 Salt Ayre
Waste Disposal and
Recycling Centre, mid-
way between
Morecambe and
Lancaster

FIGURE 6.1.4 Typical
rural landscape:
'Lonsdale', North
Lancashire

FIGURE 6.1.5 Heysham
'A' and 'B' Nuclear
Power Stations, near
Morecambe

Smell a foul blight on our city says MP

By Richard Machin

Lancaster's MP has made a passionate appeal for an end to foul smells from Nightingale Hall Farm, which he says are blighting the historic city.

Hilton Dawson was speaking at a public inquiry considering an appeal by Nightingale Hall Farm bosses against tough new operating conditions imposed by the city council. Among those conditions is a requirement that there be no offensive odours beyond the animal processing plant's boundary.

Mr Dawson told the inquiry that the vast majority of people in Lancaster considered the smell from Nightingale Hall Farm to be the single biggest problem with the city. He explained: 'People can't sit out in their gardens on fine days, patients in hospitals have to put up with the smell, children in local schools have to play out in it and people tending graves in the cemetery are subjected to it.

Mr Dawson urged the inquiry to uphold the condition banning smells beyond the process boundary, saying it would have 'profound benefits' for the whole of Lancaster.

Earlier in the proceedings lawyers representing Fats and Proteins claimed there were not enough 'exceptional circumstances' in Lancaster to warrant a ban on foul odours from Nightingale Hall Farm. The company's legal team argued that Nightingale Hall Farm was a model of good practice in the rendering industry and it would be unreasonable to impose the new conditions.

In his opening remarks barrister Martin Kingston, representing Fats and Proteins, said the company has invested in the very best available equipment and pointed out that the Secretary of State had ruled that conditions restricting smells should only be imposed in 'exceptional circumstances', and that by definition this should 'rarely arise'.

One of the only plants in the country where such a smell condition has been successfully applied is at Smith Bros in Hyde, Cheshire, where the factory is right in the midst of houses.

Mr Kingston argued that complaints about smells from Nightingale Hall Farm were unreliable and orchestrated by campaigners, claiming they sometimes came when the plant wasn't even in operation and when the wind direction meant smells couldn't affect residential areas.

Environmental consultant Mr William Bell claimed there was an 'extremely efficient' odour reduction system in place at Nightingale Hall Farm and the city council's bid to impose smell conditions was a clear attempt to close the plant down.

Mr Bell illustrated his point by saying that at no time during the past 20 years had any action been taken against Fats and Proteins under environmental nuisance legislation.

Cross-examining Mr Bell the city council's barrister, Eric Shannon, argued against the claim that the numbers of smell complaints was an unreliable indicator, adding that more than 700 complaints in the last two years couldn't be dismissed.

Mr Shannon took particular issue with Mr Bell's claims that at the time of certain complaints the wind speed and direction meant the smells couldn't have come from the plant.

Mr Shannon argued that Mr Bell's data on wind speed and direction was taken from equipment in Blackpool and therefore couldn't be applied to Lancaster with any degree of accuracy. He continued: 'You would have had as much success predicting wind direction in this particular part of Lancaster by asking Gipsy Rose Lee on Blackpool sea front.'

Residents too embarrassed to invite visitors

RESIDENTS angered by foul smells from Nightingale Hall Farm left a government inspector in no doubt about the strength of feelings in local communities as they addressed a special evening session of the public hearing.

More than 20 people got to their feet to tell their stories of years living with the stench.

They told of being too embarrassed to invite friends into their homes, of being driven indoors from their gardens by the sickening smell, of having to keep all their windows closed on hot days, of washing being impregnated with the odour and of children having to cover their faces while walking to school.

JOHN COUSINS, of Borrowdale Road, said he'd suffered the smell for 10 years: 'It's impossible to stop in the garden some times or sleep at night without closing all the windows.'

Chairman of the Fight the Furnace campaign group **RICHARD DOW**, of Derwent Road, said it was 'laughable' for the company to suggest it is only a small group of residents who oppose the plant: 'This is not some sort of conspiracy, it's the people of Lancaster and we are sick of suffering the smells from Nightingale Hall.'

RAY HILL, of Whitbarrow Square, told how his 30th wedding anniversary had been disrupted last summer as friends and family were driven inside from their barbeque celebration by 'the most putrid, wretched stink imaginable.'

DR JOHN NORTH of Rydal Road told how psychiatric patients at Ridge Lea were unable to walk in the hospital grounds because of the smell.

ANDREW KING of Borrowdale Road said it was the 'ultimate embarrassment' not being able to invite people to his own home for fear they may be subjected to the foul smell.

LAWRIE DOW, a pupil at Christ Church CE Primary School, which backs on to the plant boundary, said he and his friends had seen rats and debris from the plant in their school nature reserve.

IAN SPENCE of Windermere Road said his work took him to factories and industrial premises on a daily basis, but never had he come across such a revolting smell.

SUE AUSTEN of Derwent Road described the smell as a 'sickly, pungent odour'. As a new mother she said she did not want her child growing up with the smell and being made physically sick or being forced to play indoors during the summer.

KATHERINE BEALE of Quernmore Road said OFSTED inspectors at Christ Church school had commented on the foul smells and warned that if Nightingale Hall Farm's appeal against the smell condition was upheld it would give them carte blanche to ruin the community.

DR PHILIP BATTY, a GP in Lancaster and chairman of the Pediatric Asthma Group, said he found it completely unsatisfactory that he visited patients suffering had asthma attacks in Freehold and Ridge Estates but they couldn't open the windows for fresh air because of the smells from Nightingale Hall Farm.

Source: *Lancaster Guardian*, 27 March 1998

FIGURE 6.1.6 Source: LANCASTER GUARDIAN, 27 March 1998

Morecambe is a traditional British seaside resort and retirement centre, renowned for its stunning sunsets over the bay and Lakeland Fells to the north west of it. Neighbouring Heysham, a key container port and Irish Sea ferry terminal, is a quaint village having some interesting relics of early Christianity. The tidal expanse of Morecambe Bay provides one of Britain's most important natural habitats and the Wildfowl Trust's bird sanctuary at Leighton Moss is only a short distance to the north of the map extract area. Lancaster is a thriving university town, whose rich and varied history can still be traced through its intact medieval castle and later 'period' buildings. The adjacent rural areas are gently undulating pastureland – the result of widespread glacial deposition – some of which includes classic examples of drumlin swarms (Figure 6.1.3).

STUDENT ACTIVITY 6.1

1 Having first located each of the following map features at their given grid reference positions, study the land-use pattern around each location in preparation for undertaking Questions 2 and 3:
■ Salt Ayre Waste Recyling and Landfill Site (mainly in the southern half of square 4562) shown in Figures 6.1.1 and 6.1.4
■ Heysham 'A' and 'B' nuclear power stations (mainly in square 4059) pictured in Figure 6.1.5;
■ the animal offal rendering plant at Nightingale Hall Farm (the unnamed building at GR 489617) located in Figure 6.1.6 and the subject of the newspaper article (Figure 6.1.7).
2 Select any one of the three features listed in Question 1, then draw a fully-annotated sketch map to show both its location and the surrounding land-uses. Your 'annotation' task is to add *detailed* labels which not only *identify* the surrounding types of land-use, *but also give some indication of the likely environmental impact of your chosen feature upon them*. When doing this, use the 1:50 000 map extract and the other listed resources as fully as possible; you should also utilise the knowledge and skills which you acquired when working through the sets of activities in the previous units.
3 Make full *written* assessments of the likely environmental impact of the other two listed features on their local areas – again using information derived from the appropriate resources in this unit as well as your existing knowledge of the 'pollution' themes involved.
4 Use a wide range of techniques to investigate any likely pollution hazards within either your own school/domestic locality or another area with which you are very familiar. In addition to identifying these hazards, you should also attempt to propose realistic strategies for overcoming them. Your tutor is likely to provide some measure of guidance with regard to your chosen pollution themes, as well as the ways in which your project might best be researched and presented. Whatever your choice of locality, however, you should refer to transport-related pollution in some detail, and may find it helpful to up-date yourself on current local and national government policies by using the Internet and local resources such as the reference library.

7

EXAMINATION PREPARATION

7.1 A revision strategy

As questions are merely combinations and permutations of a quite limited range of ideas and activities, it is wise to adopt a revision strategy which recognises this fact. One possible strategy requires the student to sub-divide the syllabus content into distinct blocks of knowledge, then *tag* each block with a short-list of its possible applications in the examination situation. Doing this provides added flexibility in the use of learned information and concepts; it also makes the task of answer-planning much easier.

This revision strategy can best be illustrated by applying it to units of the book. Unit 4.6 provides a good example of 'block tagging', but the list below is by no means exhaustive:
■ different forms of marine pollution;
■ the 'cocktail effect' – the combined impact of individual pollutants reacting with each other;
■ the influence of both natural and physical factors in determining the form of a major hydrological

store and its ability to cope with pollutant inputs;
■ international responses to marine pollution;
■ the impact of an NGO pressure group (Greenpeace), whose strength lies in its independence of official government agencies;
■ the tendency of governments/industrialists to initiate environmental strategies *only when compelled to do so*, e.g. by the force of public opinion.

STUDENT ACTIVITY 7.1

1 Note down the six suggested applications of Unit 4.6 listed above, then add at least a further two applications of your own.
2 Devise five further 'application lists', each to be based on single units in Parts 1–5 of the book; you are strongly advised to select only one unit from each part.

7.2 Structuring examination answers

Many examination questions are worded so as to test a candidate's powers of interpretation as well as his/her knowledge of the subject matter. Whilst they may appear to offer a daunting and almost infinite variety of challenges, questions are merely selections of standard elements, each element designed to convey a crucial 'signal' to the candidate. The most common types of elements are those which provide:
■ *command words* such as *discuss, compare, contrast* and *justify*. A clear understanding of their meanings is so important that a set of definitions for the more common commands is given below;
■ *spatial guidance* such as *local, regional, international* or *global* contexts. *At different scales/at a range of scales* indicates that you must consider situations at more than one spatial level (e.g. within both the local and regional contexts). Spatial guidance may also include 'global components'

such as *biosphere* and *hydrosphere*. Other common spatial guidelines are:
the developed countries/world (also *'The North'* and *EMDCs*) – to indicate the wealthier regions
less developed countries/world (also *'The South'* and *LEDCs*) – to indicate somewhat poorer regions;
■ *topic coverage limitations* such as *marine* pollution;
■ *statements to be debated*. You are normally expected to debate both the 'pros' and the 'cons' of the chosen statement, then add a brief conclusion which summarises their relative strengths.

It is sound practice for candidates at all examination levels to devote the first few minutes of allotted question time to planning the basic structure of their response. This 'answer plan' can take the form of a short-list of notes, which can then be added to as additional 'fresh' ideas come to mind.

STUDENT ACTIVITY 7.2

1 Prepare 'outline answer plans' for the following questions:
(a) 'Pollution problems rarely respect international boundaries'. Discuss this statement with reference to *either* air pollution *or* water pollution.
(b) Debate the assertion: 'That the nature of the major pollutants has changed significantly during the course of the twentieth century'.

(c) With reference to case studies of your own choice, justify the assertion: 'That environmental protection measures are usually prompted by externally-imposed pressures rather than self-motivation on the part of government agencies'.

7.3 Specimen examination questions

Note: Most A and AS level questions carry either 20 or 25 marks. Any specimen examination questions reproduced below without mark allocations in brackets may, therefore, be assumed to be part-questions carrying fewer marks.

1 Explain why 'sustainable development' has become such a necessary focus for development policies. (25)   *London 'B'*

2 'Those who create pollution must pay for the consequences'. Discuss this statement with reference to a range of case studies you have studied from both MEDCs and LEDCs. (25)
London 'B'

3 Describe and explain the effects on the environment of areas which you have studied which could result from attempting to raise agricultural productivity by the increased use of chemical fertilisers.   *Cambridge Modular*

4 Consider the conflicts of interests that may arise between developed and developing countries over the issue of bio-diversity and the 'rights' of the developing countries to a greater control over the benefits from the exploitation of their natural resources.   *Oxford and Cambridge*

5 Describe and account for the distinctive features of urban climates. (25)   *ULEAC*

6 With the aid of appropriate examples, describe and account for the ways in which an urban area in temperate latitudes may modify the climate over and around the city. (25)   *AEB*

7 (a) Explain the circumstances that may lead to high levels of atmospheric pollution in urban and industrial areas.
(b) Why have efforts to reduce this pollution met with only limited success?
Answer with reference to specific examples from **either** the *developed* **or** the *less developed* (developing) world.   *Oxford and Cambridge*

8 Show, with examples at different scales, how the rapid expansion of tourism can create serious environmental stress.   *Oxford and Cambridge*

9 Explain the background to the increasing concern for the impact of human activity on atmospheric processes. What are the reasons for this concern? (25)   *AEB*

10 Outline some of the alternative sources of energy available in the world today and show how they may provide an attractive option for some countries.   *Cambridge Linear*

11 With reference to case studies at different spatial scales, discuss why the development of new energy resources frequently creates intense debate and conflict.   *Cambridge Linear*

12 Using examples:
(a) Describe the environmental disbenefits of manufacturing industry at different scales. (13)
(b) Explain how environmental considerations can influence the location of manufacturing industry.
(12)   *Oxford and Cambridge*

13 With reference to examples at several scales, show how the interaction between population and resources can have adverse environmental consequences.   *Oxford and Cambridge*

14 'Pollution does not respect international boundaries'. Discuss this statement with reference to *either* air *or* water pollution. (25)   *London 'B'*

15 'Pollution is a largely unavoidable and inevitable consequence of economic development'. Discuss this statement with reference to a range of case studies you have studied. (25)   *London 'B'*

16 Comment on the economic and environmental consequences of the tendency for manufacturing industry to be concentrated on the coast in many developing countries.   *London 'A'*

INDEX

Intro. – reasons for choice of regions i.e.
1. spatial breadth (covers much of W. Europe)
2. breadth of topic coverage (i.e. air + 2 water-related themes + wide range of causes/processes/immediate effects/long-term repercussions

AIR POLLUTION – in much of Western Europe

– causes/locations of causes (? powerstations, cars/ UK)
– processes/reasons for widespread nature (? reactions in atmosphere/prevailing winds/wind changeability)
– effects/locations of effects (? lakes. forests/ Scandinavia, Germany)
– emphasise scale of region affected

RIVER-BORNE POLLUTION – R. Rhine

– causes/locations (? industry, agriculture, conurbations/Ruhr, Basle explosion)
– reasons for widespread dispersal (? length of R. Rhine/ river basin includes most of W. Europe/speed of flow/N. Sea pollution input)
– effects (? fish losses/size of claims against companies)
– regional response (? Rhine Plan)

MARITIME POLLUTION – North Sea

– causes/locations (? range of inputs – nuclear, oil, sewage etc/UK, shipping routes, river inputs – name them!)
– processes/reasons for dispersal (? see currents, winds again!, 'cocktail effect')
– effects/locations of effects (? impact on fish, cost implication)
– scale of impact (? N.S. Conferences, monitoring needs)

Conclusion Emphasise again inter-regional impact of all 3 above studies/summary statement indicating truth of question's assertion)

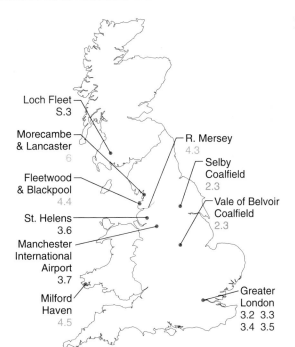

Case study locations: Britain

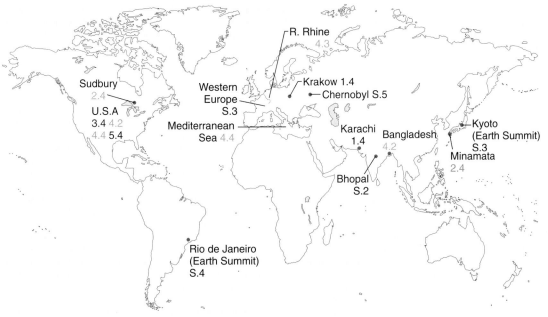

Case study locations: Rest of the world

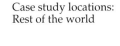

GLOSSARY

Section 1

Acid rain Precipitation which contains dilute concentrations of (chiefly) sulphuric and nitric acids

Carcinogen Substance capable of initiating cancers

Criteria Reasons for making a particular decision

Gross Domestic Product (GDP) Total value of all the goods produced and services provided *within* a country

Gross National Product (GNP) is similar to GDP, but also includes income from certain *external* goods and services (e.g. shipping and insurance)

Life expectancy Average number of years from birth that a person may reasonably expect to live

National (external *or* foreign) debt Total borrowings incurred by a country through loans from other countries or international banks and organisations

Non-governmental organisation (NGO) Organisation which concerns itself with environmental issues but is neither funded nor controlled by a national government

Primate city Largest city (by far) in a country or region

Prime mover Chief instigator of a new development; can be governments, companies, NGOs or individual persons

Section 2

Agribusiness Farming systems increasingly based on scientific and business principles so as to maximise profits

Biological oxygen demand (BOD) Amount of dissolved oxygen required by marine decomposers to break down organic materials such as effluent under a given set of circumstances (e.g. water volume and temperature)

Eutrophication Physical, chemical and biological changes within a body of water as a result of nutrient enrichment

Fertiliser Organic or manufactured soil additive whose purpose is to increase yields of agricultural produce

Fungicide Toxic preparation designed to eradicate fungal diseases able to impair the growth or productivity of crops

Green revolution Collective term applied to a range of post-war measures (e.g. irrigation and the use of higher-yielding crop strains) adopted by LEDCs to increase agricultural output

Herbicide Crop application whose purpose is to control the growth of competitive weeds

Insecticide Chemical designed to combat insects having the potential to restrict agricultural production

Organic farming Form of farming using only natural instead of chemical applications to enhance production

Overburden Over-lying rock layer(s) which have to be removed during open-cast mining operations to access the sought mineral(s) below them

Particulate solid Term used to refer to atmospheric constituents which are in solid rather than gaseous form

Point source Precise location where one or more pollutants are discharged into the environment (as opposed to **non-point sources**, which are much larger areas, such as fields, from which pollutants are discharged)

Section 3

Ambient Concerning outdoor environmental conditions

Brownfield site Area of land which has previously been subjected to urban/industrial development

Concentric model An attempt to generalise settlements' tendency to develop similar patterns of land-use with increasing distance from the core zone

Footloose industry Industry whose factory locations are dependent upon the availability of an adequate **infrastructure** of local services (especially power supplies and road access) rather than the availability of raw materials

Greenfield site Area of land which has *not* previously been used for urban/industrial development

Landfill Disposal of unwanted solid material (e.g. domestic refuse) on land set aside for that purpose

Leaching Process by which dissolved material (e.g. plant nutrients) is removed from topsoil layers by percolating water

Overspill population Group of people needing to be re-housed outside their original settlement as a result of urban renewal schemes taking place within it

Photochemical smog Form of smog caused by the action of sunlight on trapped vehicle emission gases following a temperature inversion of the lower atmospheric layers

Primary pollutant Pollutant which affects an ecosystem without itself having been changed from its original form

Rural-urban (rurban) fringe Zone along a settlement boundary; the interface between town and country

Secondary pollutant Pollutant formed when primary pollutants react with each other and/or constituent elements of the local natural environment

Sector model An attempt to generalise settlements' tendency to develop similar land-uses along linear sectors linking the core and fringe zones (e.g. along a river course or main road)

Smog A pollutant combination of smoke and fog

Temperature inversion Atmospheric condition in which air temperatures increase instead of decreasing with greater height above ground level

Topography Pattern of surface features (especially natural features such as land height and shape) in an area

Urbanisation Process by which the *proportion* of people living in towns and cities increases faster than in rural areas

Urban sprawl Tendency for suburban areas to spread outwards into adjacent countryside

Zone of transition Urban zone subject to fundamental change in land-use and/or quality of buildings

Section 4

Crude oil (petroleum) Oil in an unprocessed state

Economy of scale Principle by which average costs (e.g. of production and transportation) tend to be significantly lower in larger-scale operations

Longevity Tendency to reach (increasing) old age

Pathogen Organism capable of producing disease

Quality of life An indication of a community's overall standard of basic provisions such as food intake, clothing and housing

Refinery Processing plant in which crude oil is distilled into a range of by-products

Section 5

Biological Diversity (biodiversity) Concerns the number, variety and variability of living organisms and their habitats

Global warming The raising of average global temperatures due to the greenhouse effect

Greenhouse effect Process that traps heat in the troposphere (lower atmosphere). Some of the heat which would normally be radiated back from the earth's surface towards outer space is absorbed by water vapour, carbon dioxide and ozone. As the concentrations of these atmospheric gases rise, the amount of heat absorbed results in increased air temperatures

Ozone depletion Loss of ozone from with the ozone layer (15–20 km above the earth's surface) due to the use of chlorofluorocarbons (CFCs) in refrigerators, air conditioning systems, spray cans and insulation materials. CFC gas appears likely to remain in the atmosphere from 60 to 400 years. In accordance with the Montreal Protocol of 1987, all countries have agreed to phase out CFCs completely by the year 2010

Primary product Product which is a major source of income for the producer country. Primary products are especially important in LEDCs and are usually within the **primary sector** industries of farming, fishing, forestry, mining and quarrying

Rapidly industrialising nation A former LEDC whose GDP has recently risen to a significantly higher level – due to widespread industrialisation and less dependence on primary industries